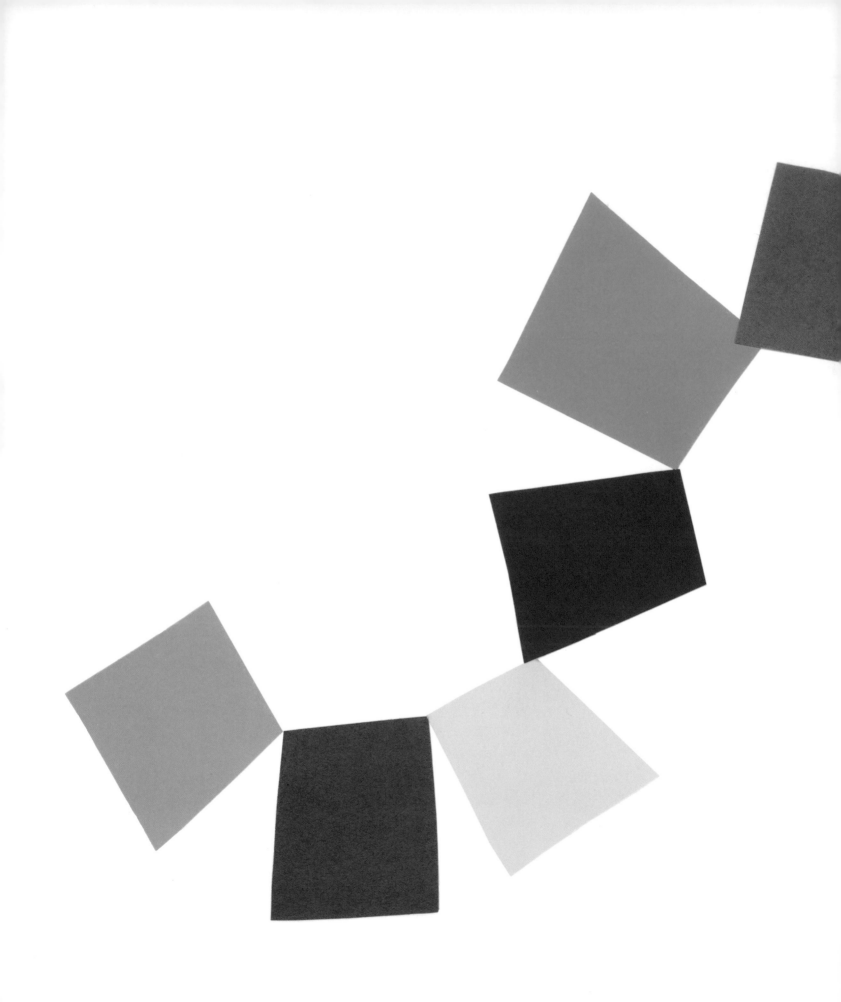

GET INTO ART

SUSIE BROOKS

KINGFISHER
LONDON & NEW YORK

KINGFISHER
LONDON & NEW YORK

Copyright © Macmillan Publishers International Ltd 2013, 2014, 2015, 2018, 2023
Text and project material Copyright © Susie Brooks 2013, 2014, 2015, 2018, 2023

First published 2023 in the United States
by Kingfisher
120 Broadway, New York, NY 10271
Kingfisher is an imprint of
Macmillan Children's Books, London
All rights reserved.

Edited by Catherine Brereton and Polly Goodman
Designed by Peter Clayman and Tony Fleetwood
Cover design by Peter Clayman
Project photography by Peter Clayman
Picture research by AME Picture Research

ISBN 978-0-7534-7982-7

Distributed in the U.S. and Canada by Macmillan,
120 Broadway, New York, NY 10271

Library of Congress Cataloging-in-Publication data has been applied for

Previously published as four separate titles: *Get into Art: Animals* (2013);
Get into Art: People (2013); *Get into Art: Places* (2014); *Get into Art: Stories* (2015)

Kingfisher Books are available for special promotions and premiums.
For details contact:
Special Markets Department, Macmillan
120 Broadway, New York, NY 10271.

For more information please visit:
www.kingfisherbooks.com

EU representative: 1st Floor, The Liffey Trust Centre
117-126 Sheriff Street Upper, Dublin 1 D01 YC43

MIX
Paper | Supporting
responsible forestry
FSC® C116313

CONTENTS

PICTURE THIS

Everything you see could become a work of art.
Just look at the world all around you! Some artists create artworks to remember people by or to illustrate a story. Others capture feelings or actions, or **an idea from their imagination**. The great thing is that artists can bring their work to life in many ways.

See how people, animals, places, and stories have inspired famous artists—then **let them inspire you, too!**
Each page of this book will tell you about a work of art and the person who created it. At the end of each section, you'll find projects based on the artworks. Don't feel that you have to copy them exactly. Half the fun of art is exploring your own ideas!

GETTING STARTED

A checklist at the start of each **set of projects will tell you what you need,** but it's a good idea to read through the project steps before you begin. There are also some handy tips on the next page . . .

Always have a **pencil** and **eraser** handy. Making a rough **sketch** can help you plan a project and see how it's going to look.

PICK YOUR PAINT . . .

Acrylic paints are thick and bright—they're great for strong colors or for textures such as hair. **Poster paints** are cheaper than acrylics but are still bright. Use them when you need a lot of paint.

Watercolors give a thinner coloring—try them over oil pastel or crayon or draw on them in ink.

Use a mixture of thick and thin **paintbrushes**. Have a glass jar or plastic cup of water ready to rinse them in, and a **palette** or paper plate for mixing paint.

TRY PASTELS . . .

Oil pastels have a bright, waxy look, like crayons. **Soft pastels** can be smudged and blended like chalk.

acrylic paint

Lay some newspaper on your surface before you start to paint!

watercolor paint

acrylic paint

sponged paint

For painting, use thick **drawing** or **watercolor paper**—anything too thin will wrinkle. **Pastel paper** has a rough surface that holds on to the color.

Collect a range of **colored papers and card stock** for collages and 3D models.

oil pastels

soft pastels

Ready to start? Let's **get into**

art!

Look around at home for other art materials. Useful things include sponges, rags or cloths, toothpicks, drinking straws, scissors, glue, string, roller brushes, and Bubble Wrap.

PEOPLE

VERTUMNUS

Giuseppe Arcimboldo *about* 1590

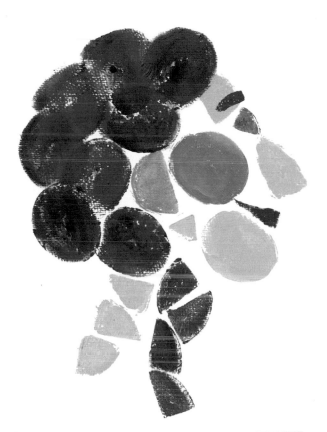

It could be a person—or a pile of fruits, vegetables, and flowers!

Arcimboldo has cleverly mixed two sides of nature in this fascinating portrait of an emperor.

Plant person

Emperor Rudolf II was used to having his portrait painted—but not with pea-pod eyelids and a pear-shaped nose! Fortunately, he had a sense of humor, and he loved Arcimboldo's witty work. Here he is dressed up as Vertumnus, Roman god of the seasons. His face is recognizable, even though it's made up of plants!

Arcimboldo was an excellent painter of nature. He also liked tricks and illusions. In this portrait he played with textures, painting lips as shiny cherries and a beard as a bristly sweet chestnut. One cheek is a rosy apple and the other a juicy peach. The ear is jokily shown as an ear of corn! What other fruits and vegetables can you see?

Plants weren't the only things that Arcimboldo turned into heads. In a painting called *Air* he chose birds; *Earth* was a head made of animals; *The Cook* was a platter of meat; and *The Librarian* was a pile of books. Some of his heads look like ordinary still lifes until you turn them upside down!

WHO WAS ARCIMBOLDO?

Giuseppe Arcimboldo was born in Italy in about 1526. He began his career designing cathedral windows and then went on to work for the imperial (royal) family in Austria. He designed costumes and festival sets and painted realistic portraits—but none of these had as much of an impact as his imaginative fruity heads!

THE CLOWNS

Albert Gleizes 1917

These swirling, spinning shapes are enough to make you dizzy!
Gleizes brings the thrill of a circus act to life in his colorful painting of two clowns.

In a spin
Can you make out the clowns' faces and hats? If you follow the dark lines, you might see their bodies, legs, and an arm or two—but these aren't the focus of the picture. Gleizes has painted them in a whirlwind of curved shapes that remind us of cartwheels and tumbles. They make our eyes jump around the scene as if we're watching acrobats on a stage!

Gleizes wanted to capture the experience of being at a circus. He chose loud, lively colors and a jumbled effect that makes everything seem to move. The shapes and patterns clash together like noisy cymbals. Some parts shimmer in the bright light. Gleizes even mixed sand into some of his paint to give it a character of its own!

This style of painting is known as Cubism because it's based on geometric shapes. Notice the top clown's face—it has pointed corners and seems to look forward and sideways at the same time! The Cubists liked to show things from many different angles, not just a single viewpoint. They broke up what they saw or remembered and rearranged it in exciting ways.

WHO WAS GLEIZES?

Albert Gleizes was born in France in 1881. He worked in his father's fabric design studio before becoming a painter. He loved the buzz of cities and stage performances and wanted his art to reflect the modern world. Not only did he paint in the Cubist style, he also wrote a book about it.

DAVID

Michelangelo Buonarroti 1501–1504

Imagine a huge block of marble, taller than a double-decker bus (that's more than 30 ft./9m high!). That's what Michelangelo began with when he carved his statue of David! Almost three years later, it was complete.

Huge hero

Other artists had tried and failed to carve this enormous chunk of stone. But Michelangelo wasn't put off. He chipped away the marble to make a full human figure, about three times larger than life!

In the Bible story, David was a shepherd boy who killed the giant Goliath with a stone from his slingshot. These close-ups of the statue show his head and upper body. You can see that he looks watchful and brave. His handsome face is evenly proportioned, his brow wrinkles thoughtfully, and veins and muscles bulge under his skin. Michelangelo has created the feel of real flesh, even though it's made of solid stone!

Although Michelangelo knew about proportion, he made David's head, hands, and upper body slightly too big. This may have been because the statue was meant to stand high up on Florence's cathedral. If people saw it from below, the proportions would seem correct!

WHO WAS MICHELANGELO?

Michelangelo Buonarroti was born in Italy in 1475. Even as a boy, it was clear that he would be an incredible artist. He worked hard, studying anatomy to help him paint and sculpt the perfect human form. Michelangelo believed that there was a statue in every block of stone— he just had to set it free!

THE SCREAM

Edvard Munch 1893

Munch's style is called Expressionist because it expresses inner feelings, rather than a realistic view of the world. This figure looks neither male nor female—it's showing someone from the inside out. Munch made four versions of *The Scream*—two in pastel and two in paint. In 2012, one sold at an auction for a record $112 million!

If you could hear a painting, this one would hurt your ears! Munch has used bold colors and brushstrokes to put the piercing sound of a scream onto paper.

A scream of nature

The person in Munch's painting has a wide-open mouth—but that's not where the scream seems to come from. It's as if the sky and sea themselves are crying out, while the figure tries to block out the noise. Munch said that one day he "sensed a great, infinite scream pass through nature"— and that's where he got the idea.

Look at the marks in the painting—they swirl and ripple like echoes. The sky is an angry, loud red, and the water seems dark, deep, and cold. Munch's figure looks ghostlike, swaying as if the scream is bouncing around inside. We get a sense of terror and confusion—which is just what the artist had felt.

WHO WAS MUNCH?

Edvard Munch was born in Norway in 1863. His mother and older sister died when he was young, and Edvard was often troubled by illness. He used art to show his feelings, but his pictures shocked many people at first. Eventually he found success and grew famous for his Expressionist style.

CHILDREN'S GAMES

Pieter Bruegel the Elder 1560

Think of all the games you know— then imagine arranging them in one scene. When Bruegel made this picture he painted more than 200 children playing in at least 80 different ways!

Old-fashioned fun

Games have changed since Bruegel's time. Instead of modern toys, these children are playing with sticks, hoops, stones, and barrels. But you might recognize some activities like leapfrog, hide-and-seek, and blindman's buff. Can you see two boys on stilts, someone blowing bubbles, and a girl on a hobbyhorse?

Bruegel loved painting many little figures together. He arranged them carefully, leading our eye to every part of the scene. Each child is in a different pose, and the high viewpoint means that every single person can be seen.

WHO WAS BRUEGEL?

Pieter Brueghel was a Flemish artist, born in about 1525. He dropped the "h" from his name and became known as "the Elder" to distinguish himself from his two painter sons. In Bruegel's time, artists often painted idealized scenes. But he preferred to show the reality of ordinary peasant life.

PORTRAIT OF ADELE BLOCH-BAUER I

Gustav Klimt 1907

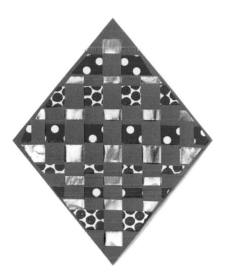

Klimt made more studies for this painting than for any other in his career. A study is a rough drawing or painting that helps an artist plan a piece of work. Klimt made many sketches in chalk or charcoal, playing around with different poses and exploring the decoration of Adele's gown.

Not many people have their portraits made in gold, but Adele Bloch-Bauer was a wealthy lady! Klimt borrowed ideas from mosaics he'd seen in Italy to create this luxurious picture.

Gleaming glamor

It was Adele's husband who commissioned the portrait—he was a fan of Klimt's work, and he had plenty of money to spend on it. The gold that you see here isn't paint but gold leaf thin, fragile sheets of real gold. As Klimt stuck it to his canvas, it wrinkled into beautiful textures.

Klimt used oil paint for the figure and the colors in her decorative dress. He loved to play with patterns and shapes arranged in a detailed patchwork style. Working like this was slow, and the portrait took almost three years. But Klimt didn't mind—he enjoyed painting this glamorous lady!

WHO WAS KLIMT?

Gustav Klimt was born in Austria in 1862, the son of a gold engraver. He began his career painting murals and decorative ceilings. Later he became known for his pictures of women. His unusual, ornamental style broke away from the traditional art of his time.

A Sunday Afternoon
On the Island Of La Grande Jatte

Georges Seurat 1884

If you're seeing spots, you're not mistaken—Seurat built up this whole scene using multicolored specks of paint!

Color clever

Hold the painting away from you—it's hard to see the dots from afar. That's what Seurat wanted. His idea was to let our eyes blend the colors, instead of his mixing them on a palette. He thought this made everything look brighter.

Seurat placed his dots carefully, using contrasting colors to make different areas stand out. The figures look almost like cutouts. There's a lot of action, but everything seems still, as if someone has pressed pause on a movie. This gives us the feel of a relaxing Sunday afternoon.

WHO WAS SEURAT?

Georges Seurat was born in France in 1859. He studied art, as well as the science of color and light—that's how he developed his style, known as Pointillism. At first people criticized his work, but this giant painting changed their minds!

GROTESQUE FACES

Leonardo da Vinci 1500s

Are these people real or imaginary? Probably a little of both! Leonardo has combined striking features with funny expressions in this set of character drawings.

Fascinating faces

Leonardo was obsessed with faces. He filled whole sketchbooks with pages like this and made notes about different features. For example, a nose could be straight, bulbous, hollow, pointed . . . the list went on! Can you think of ways he might have described eyes, mouths, chins, and necks, too?

Leonardo would search the streets for unusual faces to draw. Sometimes he followed people all day and then made sketches later. Most of his "grotesques" show old men or women with sagging skin and toothless jaws. Almost all of them face sideways, as if they don't know that they're being watched.

Leonardo made these sketches in brown ink on paper. He was always scribbling in notebooks, recording his ideas. Usually he wrote backward in mirror writing! This was probably because he was left-handed and it was easier to move his pen from right to left without smudging the ink.

WHO WAS LEONARDO?

Leonardo da Vinci was born in Italy in 1452. He lived during the Renaissance, when a lot of great art was being made. Leonardo was a scientist, inventor, writer, architect, musician, mathematician, and all-around genius, as well as being a brilliant artist! He was curious about everything, and it showed in all his work.

EGYPTIAN BURIAL MASK

Ancient Egyptian craftspeople *around* 3000 B.C.E to 1000 C.E.

This might seem too elaborate a way to dress up a dead person—but in ancient Egypt, looking good after death was important!

Forever face

The Egyptians believed that when you died, you could live on forever in the afterlife. But to get there, your body had to be preserved so your soul always had a home—and a burial mask helped with this. It meant that your soul could recognize your body, and it also gave protection in the tomb.

The type of mask depended a lot on how rich or important you were. If you were royal, it was made of gold and jewels! The main mask shown here was painted gold for a woman who had less money. Around her face is a patterned headdress, decorated with symbols of the afterlife. Right at the top is the Eye of Horus, a symbol of protection.

To preserve their dead, the Egyptians bandaged them as mummies—but first, they removed certain body parts and kept them in four jars. These jars showed the heads of the Four Sons of Horus, who you can see at the bottom of the mask above. The falcon-headed gods on each side of his sons represent Horus himself.

HOW WERE THEY MADE?

Masks like this were usually made of cartonnage—a material a little like papier-maché. They began as a mold, or cast, of the person's face. This was then painted with an idealized image rather than an accurate portrait. Gold was often used because it was the color of the flesh of the gods.

GIRL IN MIRROR

Roy Lichtenstein 1964

Lichtenstein wanted to give his work the mechanical feel of mass printing. He chose only the colors used in industrial printing: red, yellow, blue, and black on white. To create his dots, he painted through rows of holes in a metal screen. This picture is done on steel and is 3.5 ft. (1m) square.

Every picture tells a story—especially if it's in a comic strip!

Lichtenstein loved the way that comics put drama on a page, so he copied their style in his paintings.

Painting like print

Are you wondering why this girl is spotted? She isn't covered in pimples! Lichtenstein borrowed a technique called Ben Day, which was used in printing. Rows of dots would make up different colors in a comic strip. Lichtenstein created his own version on a much bigger scale.

Notice the thick black outlines in the painting. They are typical of comics, too. So is the way that Lichtenstein cropped the girl's head in close-up. Because we see just one isolated scene, we have to imagine the story. Where is she going? What is she thinking? Who is she trying to impress?

WHO WAS LICHTENSTEIN?

Roy Lichtenstein was born in the United States in 1923. He studied and taught art and tried out many styles, but it was Pop Art that made him famous. He took the bold, brash images of advertising and print and turned them into valuable paintings. Glamorous comic-book blondes were one of his favorite subjects.

LAWN TENNIS

Eadweard Muybridge 1887

These photos aren't frames from a movie—they were taken with several still cameras! Muybridge has captured the many stages of a movement so that it slowly unwinds before our eyes.

Fast photographs

In Muybridge's day, photography was very new. Few people had tackled moving subjects before. Muybridge developed a fast-shutter-speed camera that would capture movement without blurring. He sometimes lined up 24 of these cameras to shoot an action sequence!

Muybridge photographed this woman playing tennis from three angles at once. We can see her from the side, front, and back as she swings her racket. Look down each column and you'll notice that she's in the same position. Look along each row and you'll see how the racket moves. Muybridge invented a machine called a zoopraxiscope to "play" his photos quickly one after the other. It made the pictures seem to move.

WHO WAS MUYBRIDGE?

Eadweard Muybridge was born in 1830 in England, but he lived mainly in the United States. His first action photos were of a galloping horse— to settle a bet that all of its feet left the ground at the same time!

PROJECT CHECKLIST 1

These are the materials you'll need for each project in the People section.
The ones in parentheses are useful, but you can manage without them!

Food features (page 35)
fruit and vegetables, knife, paper towel, paintbrush, acrylic or poster paints,
paper plate or palette, thick white paper

Clowning around (page 36)
different colored paper, fabric scraps, cardboard, pencil, scissors, glue, (zigzag craft scissors)

Perfect proportion (page 37)
paper, pencil or pen

The Squeal (page 38)
rough-surfaced paper, pencil, soft pastels or chalk

Playful poses (page 39)
kitchen sponge, scissors, acrylic or poster paints, paper plate or palette, colored paper, paintbrush, (tape)

Patchwork patterns (page 40)
acrylic, poster and watercolor paints, ink, paper plate or palette, crayons,
oil pastels, colored paper, tissue paper, scissors, glue, paintbrushes,
scratchers (e.g. fork, drinking straw), textured surfaces (e.g. corrugated
cardboard, Bubble Wrap), plastic wrap, salt

Sunny spots (page 41)
thick white paper, pencil with an eraser on the end, acrylic or poster paints,
paper plate or palette, damp cloth

Funny faces (page 42)
paper, pencils or pens, watercolor paint or ink, pieces of patterned paper, card stock,
scissors, glue, Popsicle sticks, (tape)

Mummy mask (page 43)
paper plate, pencil, thick cardboard, scissors, white craft glue with nozzle top,
scrap paper, acrylic paints (including gold), paintbrush, paper plate or palette,
shiny colored paper (or tinfoil and felt-tip pens)

Dotted dazzler (page 44)
Bubble Wrap, sponge or roller, acrylic or poster paint, paper plate or palette, white paper,
scissors, colored paper, pencil, glue, black marker (or paintbrush and black paint)

Action snaps (page 45)
camera, friend, computer, (printer, paper, scissors, glue)

FOOD FEATURES

Experiment with fruit and vegetables to print some **foody figures!**

Cabbages and onions give a wrinkly effect.

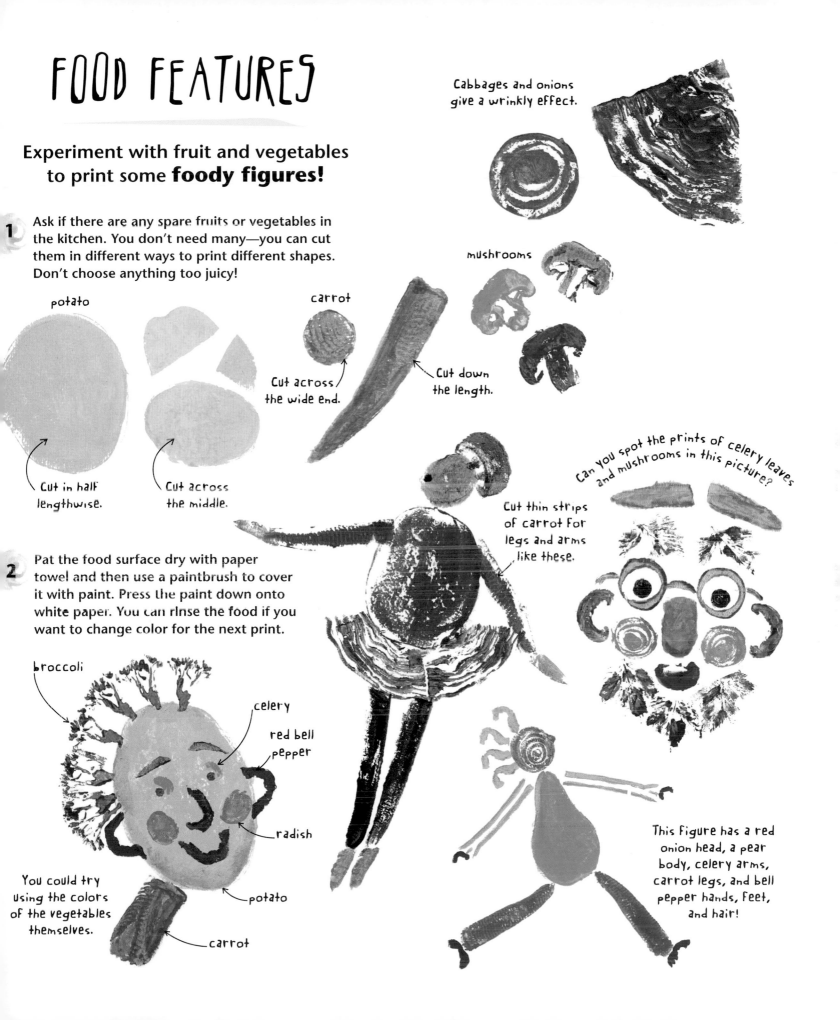

1 Ask if there are any spare fruits or vegetables in the kitchen. You don't need many—you can cut them in different ways to print different shapes. Don't choose anything too juicy!

potato

carrot

mushrooms

Cut across the wide end.

Cut down the length.

Cut in half lengthwise.

Cut across the middle.

Can you spot the prints of celery leaves and mushrooms in this picture?

Cut thin strips of carrot for legs and arms like these.

2 Pat the food surface dry with paper towel and then use a paintbrush to cover it with paint. Press the paint down onto white paper. You can rinse the food if you want to change color for the next print.

broccoli

celery

red bell pepper

radish

potato

carrot

You could try using the colors of the vegetables themselves.

This figure has a red onion head, a pear body, celery arms, carrot legs, and bell pepper hands, feet, and hair!

CLOWNING AROUND

Play around with geometric shapes to create **a Cubist-style clumsy clown collage!**

1 Think of all the shapes you could use to make up a clown, then sketch them on a piece of rough paper.

2 Collect together some different colored papers and fabric scraps such as dishtowels and felt. Using your sketch as a guide, cut out several shapes in different colors and sizes.

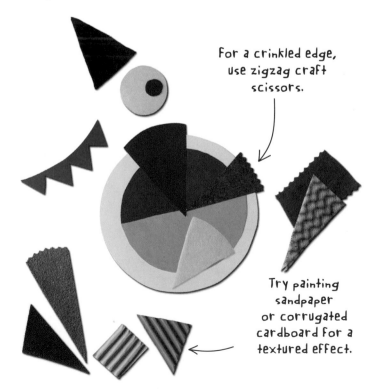

For a crinkled edge, use zigzag craft scissors.

Try painting sandpaper or corrugated cardboard for a textured effect.

3 Make a background for your collage by sticking down some large colored shapes on a piece of cardboard or posterboard. Think about the striped sides and spotlights of a circus tent!

4 Now arrange your clown shapes on the background, overlapping and angling them in interesting ways. When you're happy with your picture, glue the pieces down.

PERFECT PROPORTION

Whenever you **draw a face,** these rules will help you get it right!

1 Start with a simple upside-down egg shape. Make a dotted line lightly down the center.

2 Measure halfway down the line and draw another dotted line across. This is where the eyes go.

The pupils sit on the line.

The gap between the eyes is the same width as an eye.

3 Halfway between the eye line and the chin, draw another dotted line. This is for the bottom of the nose and ears.

The ears fit roughly between the eye and nose lines.

The nostrils reach to the inner corners of the eyes.

4 Draw a final dotted line halfway between the bottom of the nose and the chin. The mouth fits above this line.

Hair starts halfway between the eye line and the top of the head.

Don't forget the eyebrows!

The corners of the mouth reach the middle of the eyes.

Tip: use these guidelines when you're drawing an adult figure.

An average adult is 7–8 heads high.

The elbow is at waist level.

The hips are halfway down.

The wrists fall below the hips.

A hand is the size of a face.

A foot is one head-length long.

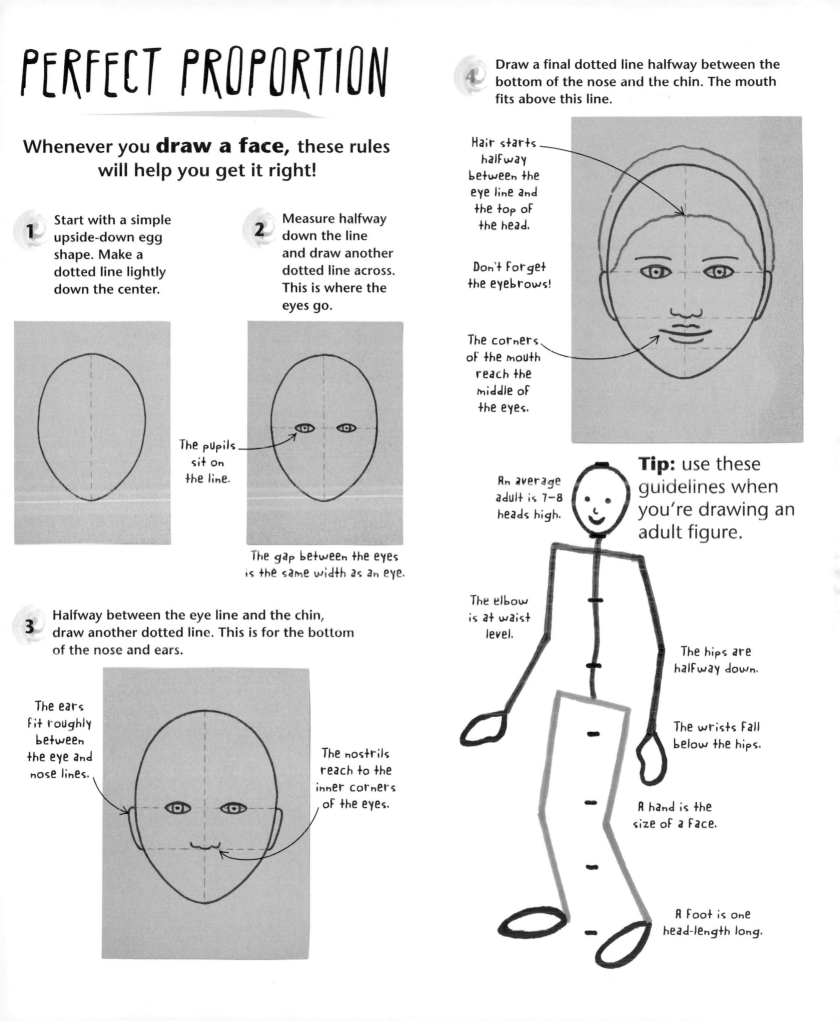

THE SQUEAL

Create a happy version of Munch's painting!

1 On a piece of rough-surfaced paper, draw a figure squealing with delight! Think about the pose and expression, but keep it simple.

Add a few background features, like the sun, fireworks, or something that makes you happy.

2 Color your figure with chalk or soft pastels. Use warm, bright colors like these.

Reds, oranges, and yellows are warm, cheerful colors.

3 Add ripples of color around the figure. Smudge together different colors with your finger to blend them.

Try to cover all of your pencil lines.

4 Continue adding swirls of bright color until your picture is complete.

PLAYFUL POSES

You can paint a page of playful figures using a kitchen sponge!

1 Start by cutting out four shapes from the sponge.

head

arm

leg

body

2 Practice printing on rough paper. Spread some thick paint onto a paper plate and dip in the sponge pieces one by one. Print the body first and then the head, legs, and arms.

3 Now try printing several figures in a row, all in different poses.

You could use a fine paintbrush to add hair, hands, or feet.

You can bend the arm and leg pieces as you print!

4 For your final painting, use a big sheet of paper or tape together some smaller ones. If you want to change the paint color, rinse and squeeze dry the sponge pieces or cut some more.

Picture your figures **running, jumping,** or **playing games.** Why not paint in a ball or a jump rope!

PATCHWORK PATTERNS

Practice different ways of making Klimt-style patterns and textures.

1 Scratch patterns into wet acrylic paint . . .

with a fork

with the end of a paintbrush

with a drinking straw

2 Lay paper onto different textures and rub with a crayon.

mesh potato bag

textured Styrofoam

wicker basket or chair

grater

3 Tear or scrunch tissue paper and glue it in a pattern onto a piece of card stock.

4 Make prints from different objects . . .

bottle tops or lids

Bubble Wrap

corrugated cardboard

5 Print from plastic wrap or lay plastic wrap onto wet ink or watercolor and peel it off when dry.

6 Draw a pattern in oil pastel and then paint over it with watercolor paint.

You get this speckled effect by sprinkling salt on the wet paint and brushing it off after the paint dries.

Can you design a costume using your patterns? Try arranging them into a shape, such as this hat.

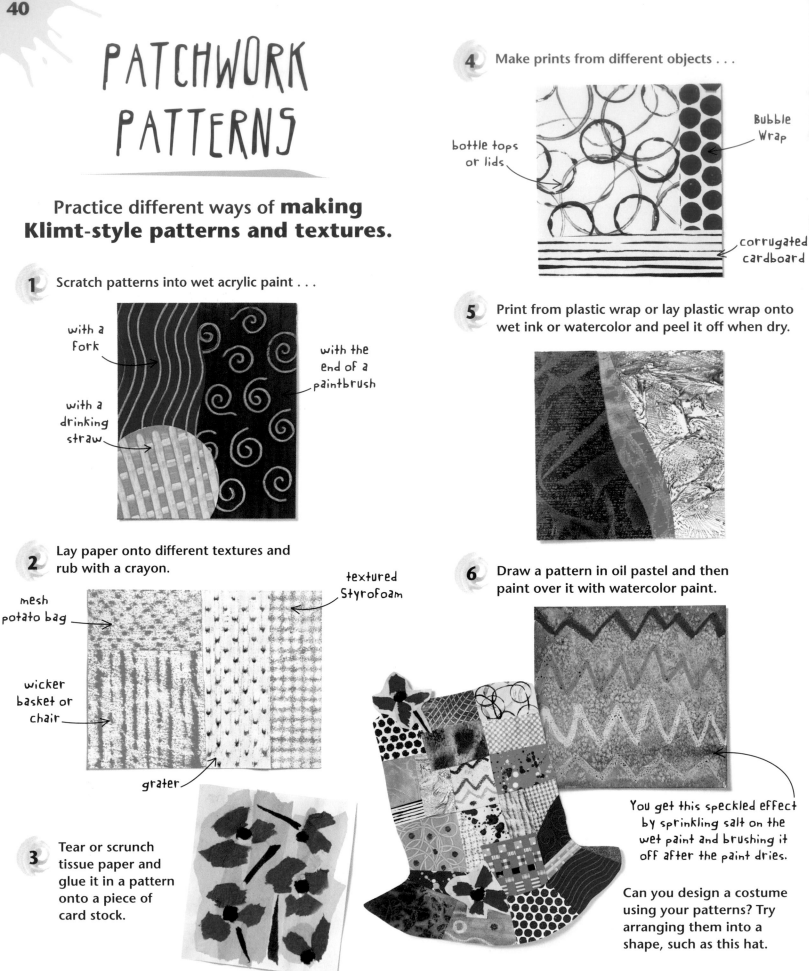

SUNNY SPOTS

Where would you like to be on a sunny Sunday? **Say it in spots!**

Sketch out a simple scene on a piece of thick white paper. Don't make it too big or it will take a really long time to paint.

Keep the figures simple. If you draw them from the back, you won't need to do their faces!

Pick a paint color to start with and squeeze some onto a palette. Use the eraser on the end of a pencil to dot the paint onto the page.

3 Gradually add dots of other colors. Wipe the eraser with a damp cloth when you change paint colors.

For light areas, dot white paint on and around the color.

For shadows, add dots of dark or contrasting colors.

For water, use dark and light blues, and white. Add dots of other colors for reflections.

4 Keep adding dots until you've finished your scene!

Think about the colors you use to paint the figures. Light colors stand out against darker ones. Contrasting colors zing out, too.

FUNNY FACES

Leonardo's sketches were a little like early cartoons. **Try doodling your own**

1 Start with just lines. Think about different expressions and how the eyes, eyebrows, and mouth change. Experiment with different shaped noses, chins, ears, and hair!

An open mouth and raised eyebrow give a shocked expression.

Downward sloping eyebrows look angry.

Curve the mouth upward and widen the eye for a happy face.

2 If you want to add shading, try using watery paint or ink.

3 Now draw some outlines on colored or patterned paper. Stick them onto card stock and then cut them out and make them into Popsicle-stick puppets!

A round mouth looks puzzled or surprised.

Glue or tape the stick to the back of the card-stock head.

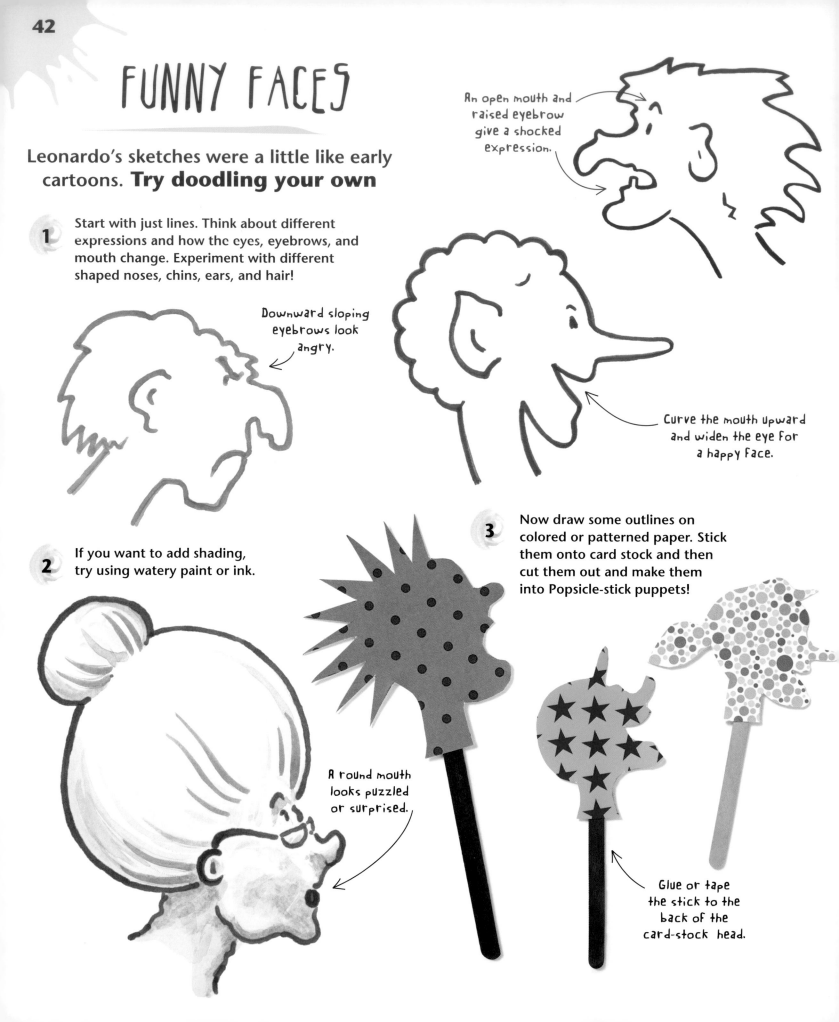

MUMMY MASK

For a quicker version of this project, miss out step 2 and just use paint for the face and other decoration.

1 On the back of a paper plate, draw an Egyptian-style face, with wide, heavily outlined eyes. Then draw around the plate on a big piece of cardboard and cut out a headdress shape like this.

Set this aside for later.

2 Now you'll need some white craft glue with a nozzle top. Practice squeezing lines of it on scrap paper and then go over the outlines on your plate. Leave it to dry overnight or until the glue is hard.

The glue will probably dry clear.

While you're waiting, you could make some decorations for the headdress (see step 4).

3 When the glue is dry, cover the face with gold or yellow acrylic paint.

Add some color to the eyes, eyebrows, and mouth.

4 Let the paint dry and then glue the plate to the headdress. Decorate the mask with pieces of shiny paper or your own painted designs.

You can cover the rim of the plate or paint it as part of the design.

These lumpy parts were done with glue, as in step 2.

Tip: If you don't have metallic paper, try coloring tinfoil with felt pens!

DOTTED DAZZLER

For this project, **imagine you're creating a close-up in a movie or comic strip**. What is your character doing or thinking? Make a sketch first if you would like.

1 To make some Ben-Day dots, spread paint over a sheet of Bubble Wrap using a sponge or roller. Lay a piece of white paper on top and press firmly, then peel it off.

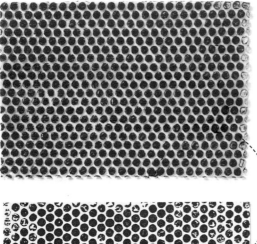

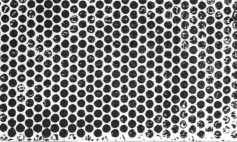

You can fill in any uneven parts with a paintbrush.

2 When the dots are dry, cut out a face. It doesn't have to be a whole face—draw it coming off the edge of the page. Then lay it on some colored paper and draw hair around it.

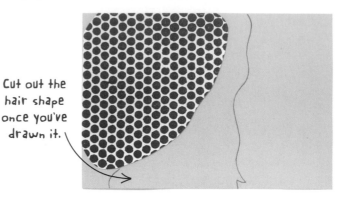

Cut out the hair shape once you've drawn it.

3 Glue the face and hair onto a colored background. Cut out eyes, a mouth, and any other details and stick them on.

You could add some extra flicks of hair.

Stick white teeth onto a red mouth shape.

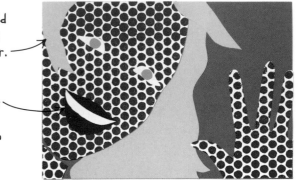

4 Finish off your picture with a marker pen or black paint. Add eyebrows, a nose, and a thick outline around all the shapes.

Try sticking on a window frame like this.

ACTION SNAPS

To photograph your own action sequences you'll need **a camera** and **a friend.**

1 Decide what movement you are going to photograph. It's best if it's something that can be done slowly. Get your friend to try moving in slow motion and holding each stage of the pose.

When you're ready to start, stand at a good distance from your subject so he or she fills the camera frame.

2 Keep the same distance between you and your friend as you photograph each stage of the action. If your model moves in one direction, you should move, too.

3 If you're photographing something quick, like a somersault, get your friend to repeat the move and press the shutter button at a different stage each time.

4 Print out your photos and arrange them in sequence— or "stitch" them together on a computer.

ANIMALS

THE SNAIL

Henri Matisse 1953

You might have to look twice before spotting the snail in this picture! There's no outline, but Henri Matisse has created the idea of a snail by arranging colored shapes in a spiral pattern.

Drawing with color

When Matisse made *The Snail*, he was 84 years old. He wasn't well enough to stand and draw, so instead he used color as his starting point. His assistants painted sheets of paper in plain colors, and then Matisse cut or tore them into shapes.

Matisse chose his colors carefully. They are not the colors of a real snail, but they are warm and bright. Matisse knew that complementary colors, such as red and green, look stronger when they're put next to each other. The way he has placed the pieces makes them zing out, as if the snail is moving. It seems to be wriggling out of the jagged orange frame!

In real life, this picture is enormous —almost 10 feet (3 meters) tall and wide! It's a collage of painted paper stuck onto white paper and then onto canvas. Matisse called this method "drawing with scissors."

WHO WAS MATISSE?

Henri Matisse was born in France in 1869. His first job was as a lawyer, but he didn't like it much. At the age of 20, he became ill and had to spend long hours in bed. His mother gave him a paint box to pass the time, and right away he knew he would become an artist! Matisse made many famous paintings in his distinctive, colorful style.

matisse 53

SUSPENSE

Sir Edwin Landseer 1861

Who is this dog waiting for? What's behind the door? Landseer wanted us to ask questions like this when he painted *Suspense*! His picture tells a story, but he leaves us to figure out what it is.

See the story

If you look closely, you'll spot some clues. There are drops of blood on the floor . . . a feather torn from a hat . . . a knight's armored gloves on the table. It seems that the dog's master has been wounded and carried through the house.

The dog sits on his haunches, staring closely at the door. We can tell that he is worried and longs to rush to his master's side. Landseer's skillful brushwork makes us feel that the animal is alive. The light glints on his anxious face, and hairs stand up on his neck. He leans forward, ready to spring up at any moment—but we can only imagine what he'll find.

WHO WAS LANDSEER?

Sir Edwin Landseer was born into a family of artists in England in 1802. He began to draw as soon as he could hold a pencil and was exhibiting work by the age of 13. Animals were his favorite subjects— he even had a breed of dog named after him! Landseer made sculptures, too, including four huge bronze lions in London's Trafalgar Square.

CRINKLY GIRAFFE

Alexander Calder 1971

This giraffe isn't going anywhere—but if you walk around it, it almost seems to move. Calder was famous for his dynamic sculptures, some of which really do move.

Animobiles

Crinkly Giraffe is made of painted metal cut into simple shapes. The flat metal looks different from different angles, so the crinkly neck seems to shift and turn. Calder made a whole series of crinkly animals like this. His wife named them animobiles!

The word animobile comes from animal and mobile—and Calder invented the mobile, too. His first one had a motor, but he soon realized that hanging shapes would move on their own. He experimented with different materials, including metal, wire, and wood. Little did he know how popular his invention would become!

In 1926, Calder made a whole circus of animals and actors out of wood, wire, cork, and cloth. He kept them in suitcases and traveled around giving performances!

WHO WAS CALDER?

Alexander Calder was born in 1898 in the United States. His father was a sculptor and his mother a painter, but Alexander studied to be an engineer. Later, he went to art school and traveled to Paris, France, to work. He used nature as his inspiration for abstract mobiles, standing "stabiles," and giant outdoor sculptures that are displayed around the world.

PEACOCK AND MAGPIE

Edward Bawden 1970

What's the first thing you notice in this picture?
Probably the peacock with its dazzling, fanned-out tail! Bawden shows us the proud character of the bird in this illustration of one of Aesop's Fables.

A telling tail

Fables are stories with a moral, which means they have a lesson to teach us. In this one, the peacock declares that he should be king of the birds. The others are impressed by his grand appearance, but the magpie questions whether he could protect the birds against eagles and other hunters. The moral is to listen to the advice of others.

Bawden cut this scene into linoleum and then printed it in ink on paper. The crisp lines make the story clear, but they are decorative, too. The yellow of the peacock catches our eye, just as it attracts the birds. Only when we look more closely do we see the magpie talking wisely to the crowd.

WHO WAS BAWDEN?

Edward Bawden was born in England in 1903. He became famous for many types of art, including book illustrations, advertising posters, murals, and metalwork furniture. He made tile paintings for the London Underground (the subway) and even designed china for passenger ships!

FISH (E59)

M. C. Escher 1942

No matter how hard you look, you won't find a gap between these fish! Escher has taken the shape of an animal and turned it into a perfect pattern. It's called a tessellation.

Tile style

Tessellation is basically tiling— every shape fits together edge to edge. Of course, it's much harder to tile an animal shape than a simple square or triangle! Escher used geometric shapes as his starting point, then changed them into curving forms. He twisted, flipped, and repeated them to make patterns.

We can see two types of fish in this picture. It's like looking through a kaleidoscope. Escher drew them on graph paper and then colored them with pencils, ink, and watercolor. He liked the idea that the pattern could go on forever, though he had to stop when he got near the edge of the page!

Escher made 137 drawings like this one. He created patterns using lizards, frogs, insects, birds, and even human shapes. His work has always fascinated mathematicians— but surprisingly, Escher struggled with math in school!

WHO WAS ESCHER?

Maurits Cornelis Escher was born in the Netherlands in 1898. His interest in linking shapes began on a trip to the Alhambra, a Moorish castle in Spain. He drew and sketched on his travels and went home to make prints of the buildings he'd seen. In his work, he loved to trick the eye and play with impossible spaces. He turned the world into a puzzling and unbelievable place!

CARNIVAL OF HARLEQUIN

Joan Miró 1924–1925

Have you ever seen things in a dream that wouldn't make sense in real life? Miró takes us to a dreamlike place in this painting of a strange but lively party!

Carnival chaos

The creatures here aren't animals as we know them, but you can probably recognize some shapes. There are winged insects, spidery forms, a fish, and two cats playing with string. Bright characters leap across the canvas, dancing to musical notes that are floating in the air.

When Miró painted this, he was poor and hungry. Perhaps that's why the main figure, the Harlequin, has a hole in his guitar-shaped stomach. He looks sad and still in this happy, playful scene. Miró said that hunger made him hallucinate, or see things that weren't really there.

WHO WAS MIRÓ?

Joan Miró was born in Spain in 1893. On a trip to Paris, France, in the 1920s, he became interested in an art style called Surrealism. He was fascinated by people's imaginations, especially children's, and became famous for his colorful paintings and sculptures that seem to come from a make-believe world.

TOTEM POLES

Wayne Alfred and Beau Dick 1991
and Ellen Neel 1955 (far left)

It's hard to imagine that these colorful carvings began life as whole cedar trees! Totem poles show the skill of traditional artists from the northwest coast of North America.

Tall stories

It can take a year to carve a totem pole! The idea is to tell a story, perhaps about an event, a legend, or people in a particular family. Each pole is a stack of characters that have special meaning in the local culture. Many animals and birds are believed to have special powers or to bring different kinds of luck.

The green-faced figure on the far left is Red Cedar Bark Man. In traditional tales, he survived a great flood and gave people the first canoe. You can see him holding a patterned boat, with the legendary Quolus bird spreading its wings above him. Quolus is the younger brother of Thunderbird, who tops the pole on the near left.

The Thunderbird brings thunder with his flapping wings and lightning with a flash of his eyes! Below him is Sea-Bear and a killer whale, then a man with a frog. Lower down we see the yellow-nosed Bakwas—"wild man of the woods"—and Dzunukwa, a child-eating giantess. They are all characters from Kwakwaka'wakw legend.

TOTEM TRADITION

Native Americans have carved totem poles for hundreds of years, but because wood rots, the oldest examples have not survived. These two were made by modern-day artists from the Kwakwaka'wakw tribe of British Columbia, Canada. You can tell they are modern because of the bright paint colors.

YELLOW COW

Franz Marc 1911

Have you ever seen a yellow cow with blue spots? Probably not! Franz Marc loved to paint from nature, but he didn't copy exactly what he saw.

Inside out

Marc said that he wanted to re-create animals "from the inside." He used colors to express different feelings. For him, yellow was cheerful, gentle, and female—like this cow, leaping happily across a sunny scene.

This is an Expressionist painting like the one on page 18. It captures a mood rather than a realistic view of the world and makes us look at things in a different way. In fact, Marc knew very well how to paint a realistic cow. He spent long hours sketching and studying animals and even taught other artists about their shape and form.

WHO WAS MARC?

Franz Marc was born in Germany in 1880, the son of a landscape painter. He took up art at the age of 20 and was soon organizing exhibitions with other Expressionist artists. Marc was fascinated by animals. He wanted to paint the world through their eyes. Sadly, he died young, fighting in World War I.

DRAGON DISH

Chinese artist 1600–1635

A snake's body, an eagle's claws, the scales of a fish . . . you can see several animals in a Chinese dragon!
These dragons are painted on a porcelain dish, surrounded by decorative swirls.

Curious creatures

Artists can have fun with dragons because they're imaginary—no one really knows what they look like! In Chinese mythology, they are often friendly, unlike the fire-breathing dragons of Europe. They are rulers of water and the weather and symbols of power and good luck.

These three dragons have lizardlike head frills and wriggling bodies that twist around the dish. Their four claws show that they are ordinary dragons—five claws would mean they belonged to an emperor. The round shapes that the dragons are chasing are magical flaming pearls. Everything is painted in a single color—cobalt blue. The artist used a fine brush for the detail and then filled in the outlines. In some parts, the color is layered to give a darker effect.

When this dish was made, artists didn't have paints like ours. Instead they used pigments— solid cakes of color that they ground into powder and mixed with liquid. This blue comes from a substance called cobalt. It has been used in Chinese pottery for more than 1,000 years.

HOW WAS IT MADE?

This type of ceramic painting is called "underglaze blue." The blue design is painted onto dried white porcelain and then coated with a clear protective glaze. Afterward it is baked, or fired, at a high temperature. This hardens the porcelain and sets the glaze.

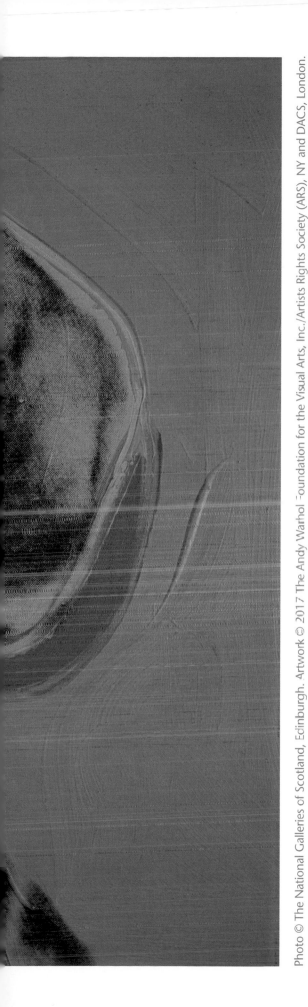

PORTRAIT OF MAURICE

Andy Warhol 1976

Andy Warhol was known for his pictures of rich and famous people—but he happily made portraits of their pets, too! This dachshund belonged to the art collector Gabrielle Keiller.

Dazzling dog

Maurice the dachshund wasn't actually blue, pink, and red! Warhol liked experimenting with bold, attention-grabbing colors—they reminded him of advertisements and modern life. He took photographs of Maurice and then worked on them back in his studio. To make this screen print, he pushed ink through a type of stencil on a silk screen.

Warhol once wrote, "I never met a pet I didn't like"—and, in fact, he had two dachshunds of his own. You can see his love of animals in this portrait of Maurice, who looks straight at us with appealing eyes.

WHO WAS WARHOL?

Andy Warhol was born in the United States in 1928. His talent for art showed from a young age, and he loved movies, photography, and cartoons. He became famous for his Pop Art inspired by advertising images and glamorous stars. Archie, one of his dachshunds, was often photographed by his side!

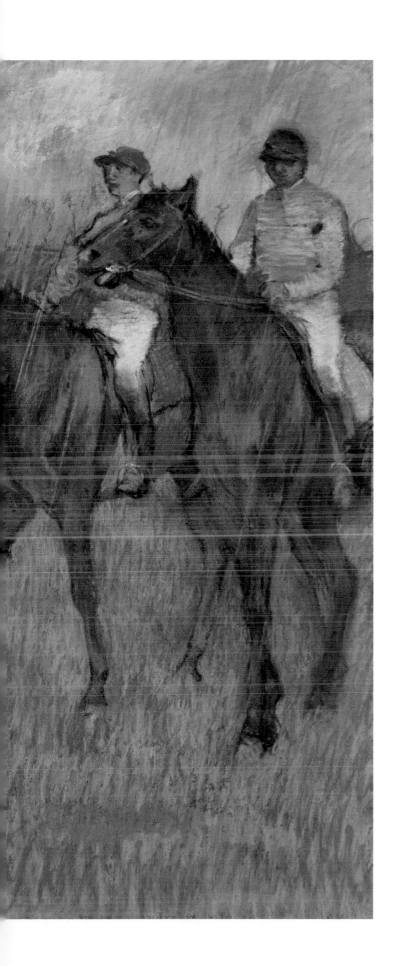

JOCKEYS IN THE RAIN

Edgar Degas *about* 1883–1886

Looking at this picture, we know just how the horses are feeling!

Degas shows us their nerves and excitement before a race, with the added restlessness of a storm.

Stormy start

Strong, colorful marks bring this pastel scene to life. Degas has drawn long streaks of blue to show the thrashing fall of rain. His diagonal strokes of green make the grass seem to sway, and the distant trees lean in the wind.

Notice how the horses are kept to one side of the drawing—some are even cut off at the picture's edge. Degas wanted us to feel the tension as the horses wait in a line. Their poses are full of movement, as if they're ready to charge ahead over the open ground.

WHO WAS DEGAS?

Edgar Degas was born in France in 1834. By the age of 18, he had created his own art studio. He loved to make pictures of everyday scenes and was fascinated by dancers and horses and how they moved. The way he cropped his figures and showed them from odd angles was seen as very daring at the time.

PROJECT CHECKLIST 2

These are the materials you'll need for each project in the Animals section. The ones in parentheses are useful, but you can manage without them!

Snip a snake (page 71)
white card stock or posterboard, brightly colored papers, scissors, glue

Furry friends (page 72)
acrylic paints, paintbrushes, sponge, toothpick

Crinkly monkeys (page 73)
colored card stock, scissors, hole punch, glue

Fabulous feathers (page 74)
thick white paper or card stock, pencil, oil pastels, acrylic paints, paintbrushes, (toothpick, teaspoon)

Fish squish (page 75)
graph paper, thin card stock, glue, ruler, pencil, scissors, tape, white paper, coloring materials (for example, markers, oil pastels, watercolor paint, paintbrushes)

Curious creatures (page 76)
thick white paper, black crayon, water-based paints, paintbrushes, (modeling clay)

Crafty totem (page 77)
cardboard tube, different colored papers, ruler, tape, pencil or chalk, scissors, (zigzag scissors), glue, stiff card stock

Moody sheep (page 78)
thick white paper, glue, sponge, bright paints, palette or paper plate, large piece of paper or posterboard, paintbrush, scissors

Dishy dragon (page 79)
paper plate, pencil, blue paint, fine paintbrush, wide paintbrush, (glitter or glitter paint)

Colorful cats (page 80)
thin card stock, pencil, scissors, thick white paper, paper clips, bright paints, sponge, colored card stock, glue, strip of card stock

Rainy racehorse (page 81)
pencil, blue pastel paper, soft pastels or chalks

SNIP A SNAKE

Matisse loved finding patterns in nature. Look at some pictures of snakes to see how they bend and curl, and then try making this snaky collage.

Your sheet can be huge, like Matisse's, or small if you have less space.

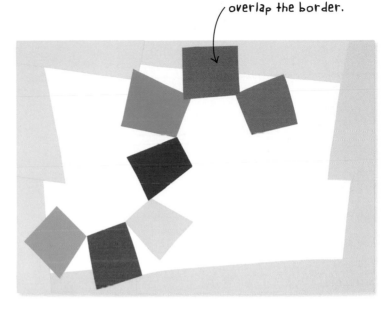

Let some pieces overlap the border.

3 Lay the shapes in a twisting pattern, thinking about which colors you are placing next to one another.

4 Move the shapes around until you're happy with your snake, and then glue them down.

straight edge here

1 Take a white sheet of card stock or posterboard as your base. Cut out some strips of colored paper—use the edges of the paper so they're straight along one side. Lay them around your card stock to make a border. Glue them down.

2 To make your snake, cut out simple block shapes from different colored pieces of paper.

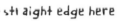

Use a big piece for the head. If you like, you can add a forked tongue!

FURRY FRIENDS

Landseer's work was very detailed, but **you can paint furry animals in different ways.** Try these!

Vary the length of the streaks.

Use the brush tip for the tail, legs, and ears.

1 Use a square-ended brush to paint the basic shape—it could be a dog like this, or your own pet or other favorite animal.

3 Now paint white highlights using short flicks of a fine brush. Use dark paint for the eye, nose, and mouth, and a few shadowy streaks under the belly.

Here are some other ways of **painting fur**.

2 With a clean brush, add downward streaks in a lighter color.

Scratch into thick, wet paint with a toothpick.

Dab dark then light paint with a piece of sponge.

CRINKLY MONKEYS

Calder turned flat materials into 3D objects. Try it yourself with these crinkly monkeys!

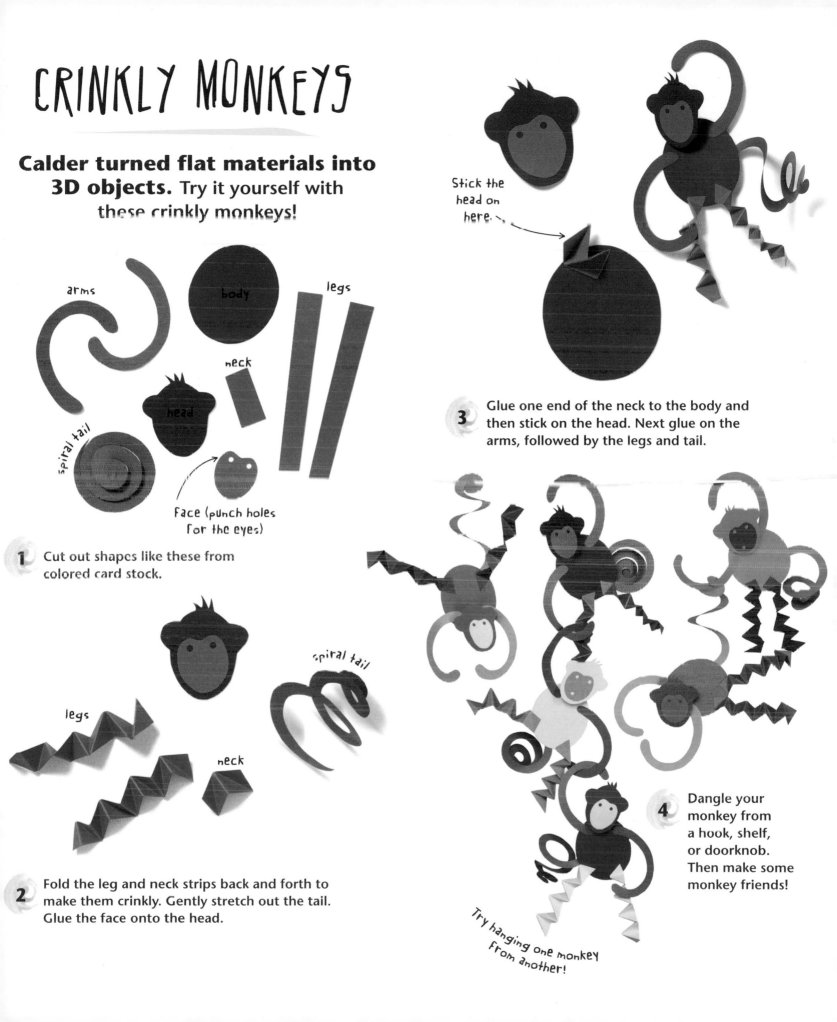

arms

body

legs

neck

spiral tail

head

face (punch holes for the eyes)

1 Cut out shapes like these from colored card stock.

spiral tail

legs

neck

2 Fold the leg and neck strips back and forth to make them crinkly. Gently stretch out the tail. Glue the face onto the head.

Stick the head on here.

3 Glue one end of the neck to the body and then stick on the head. Next glue on the arms, followed by the legs and tail.

4 Dangle your monkey from a hook, shelf, or doorknob. Then make some monkey friends!

Try hanging one monkey from another!

Try scraping into paint to create some

FABULOUS FEATHERS

1 Draw the outline of a peacock on a piece of thick paper or card stock. Start with the body and then add a big, fanlike tail.

Draw circular markings on the tail.

3 Now squeeze some dark blue and dark green acrylic paint onto a palette or paper plate. Paint over the oil pastel—try to work quickly and lay the paint on thickly.

Paint the gree tail and then th blue spots and body.

2 Color your peacock with a thick layer of oil pastel. Use light, bright colors like these.

4 While the paint is still wet, scrape feathery patterns into it. If you make a mistake, just paint over it and scrape again!

The oil pastel colors show through.

You could use the end of a paintbr

a toothpick . . .

or the end of a teaspoor

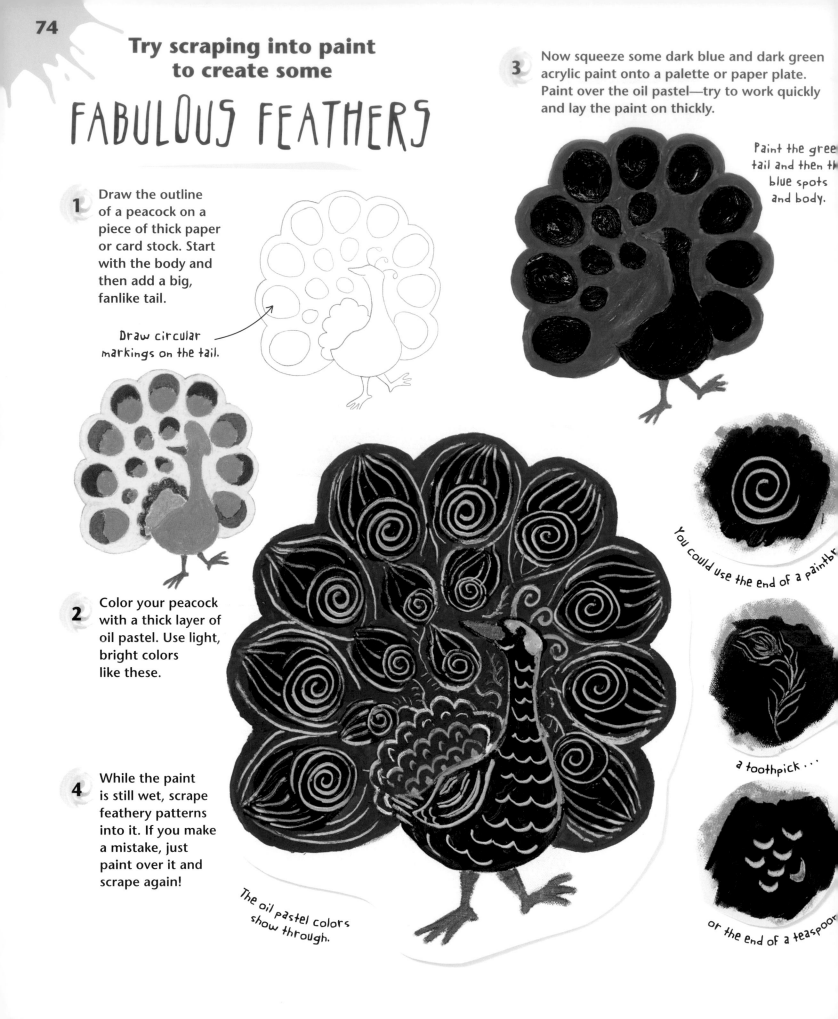

Make this simple template for an Escher-style

FISH SQUISH

1 Glue a piece of graph paper to some card stock and cut out a 2 x 2 in. (5cm x 5cm) square. Mark two triangles across opposite corners, as shown.

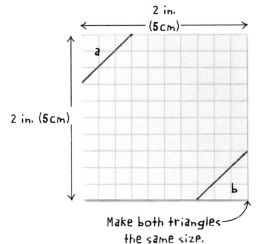

2 in. (5cm)

2 in. (5cm)

a

b

Make both triangles the same size.

2 Cut off one triangle and carefully tape it to the other side of the square, like this.

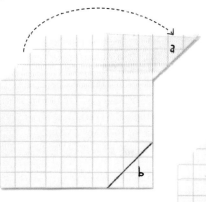

Move the triangle without turning it.

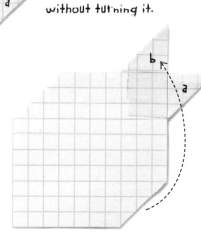

Do the same with the other triangle. Your fishy template is complete!

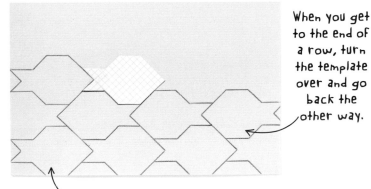

When you get to the end of a row, turn the template over and go back the other way.

Start here.

3 At the bottom of a large sheet of paper, draw around your template in pencil. Then move it along so that the tail slots into the head and draw around it again. Keep going like this!

These fish were outlined in marker, shaded with oil pastel, then washed over with watercolor paint.

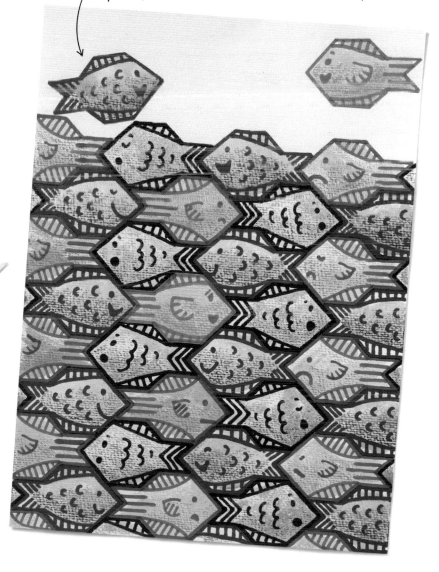

4 When you've got a full page of fish, color them in!

Let your imagination go wild with these
CURIOUS CREATURES

1 On a piece of thick white paper, draw some shapes in black crayon. Don't think about it too much—just draw!

You could use squared shapes instead of round ones.

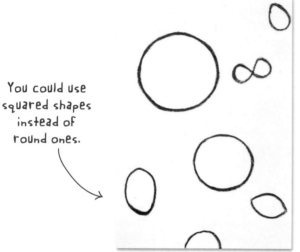

2 Now start adding lines, swirls, and other shapes. Turn your page into a circus of imaginary creatures!

Let some lines go right to the edge of the page.

You can paint right over squiggly lines like this one—the waxy crayon will show through.

3 Color in your picture with water-based paint.

Miró made sculptures, too. Try creating some **mini monsters** out of modeling clay!

CRAFTY TOTEM

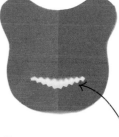

Tape the strips on the back.

height of tube

1 Cut some paper so that it's the right size to wrap around your tube. You could tape several strips together, like this.

Folded edge

Use zigzag scissors for this effect.

2 Cut out some simple animal shapes. To make them symmetrical, cut them from a folded piece of paper.

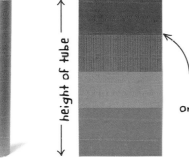

Add feathers, paws, and other shapes to the sides.

3 Glue your animals down the center of the paper. The more shapes you cut and layer, the more decorative the pole will look.

Cut slits in the top of the tube to slot the wings in.

4 Wrap your finished design around the tube and tape it on the back. For a final touch, you could make some colorful cardboard wings.

Get a feel for colours with these

MOODY SHEEP

Yellow makes a lively, happy sheep.

1 Pick a paint color and squeeze some onto a palette or paper plate. Dip a sponge in the paint and use it to paint a fluffy sheep's body.

2 Look at the color and decide how it makes you feel. Think of that mood as you paint in the sheep's head and legs.

Lilac is calm for a snoozy sheep.

This green is gloomy for a grumpy sheep.

3 Repeat steps 1 and 2 using different colors.

What colors would you use for an **angry sheep**, a **lazy sheep**, or a **startled** one?

4 Why not make a big picture with all of your moody sheep? Take a large piece of paper or posterboard and sponge paint a colorful background. Cut out your sheep and glue them on!

Transform a paper plate with your own

DISHY DRAGON

1 Sketch your dragon in pencil first. Draw the head and then a long, snakelike body and tail. Add four legs with clawed feet.

2 Use a fine brush and thick paint to cover the outline in blue. Then color it in with a wide brush and watery paint.

You can layer more color to make some areas darker.

3 Experiment with different brushstrokes before adding detail to your dragon.

Use the tip of a fine brush for delicate lines.

A flick of a brush gives scaly shapes like this.

Try a sideways dab of the brush . . .

. . . and long, sideways strokes.

4 Decorate your dragon with scales and fins. Add swirling patterns around it.

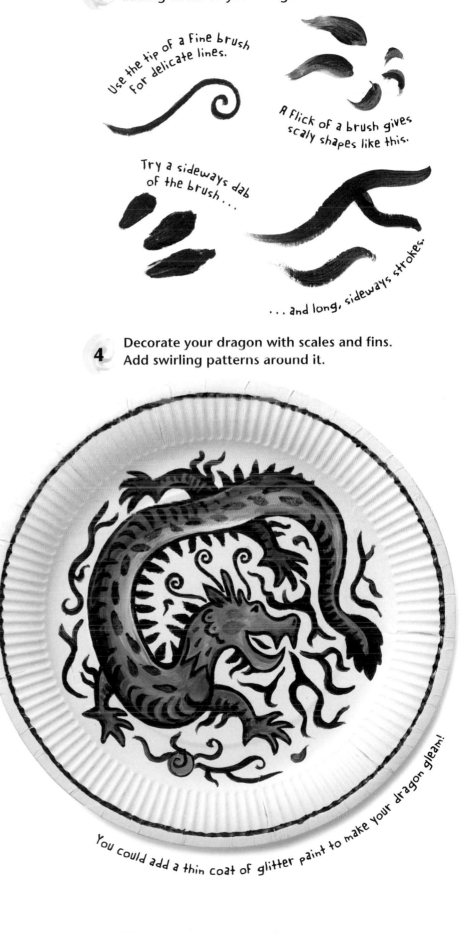

You could add a thin coat of glitter paint to make your dragon gleam!

COLORFUL CATS

Warhol's silk-screen method was complicated, but **you can get a similar effect with a simple stencil.**

1 On a piece of card stock, draw the outline of an animal and carefully cut it out. You'll end up with two stencils like these.

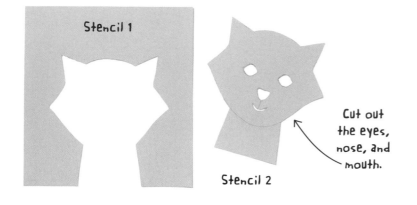

Stencil 1

Stencil 2

Cut out the eyes, nose, and mouth.

2 Lay Stencil 1 on a piece of thick paper and attach it with paper clips. Sponge yellow paint all over it.

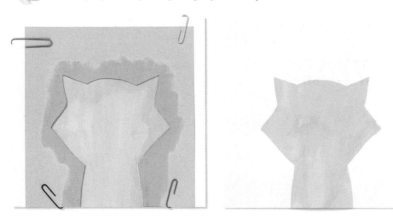

Warhol often repeated his prints in different colors. **Try making a set like this!**

3 When the paint is dry, lift the stencil and move it slightly down and to one side. Sponge red paint unevenly over it and then leave it to dry.

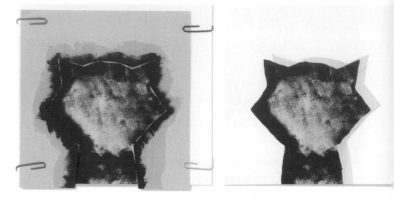

4 Now lay Stencil 2 on top of the picture and sponge blue paint over the holes. Leave it to dry, and then remove the stencil. Cut out the animal and stick it onto a colored background.

You can print whiskers by dipping the edge of a strip of card stock in paint.

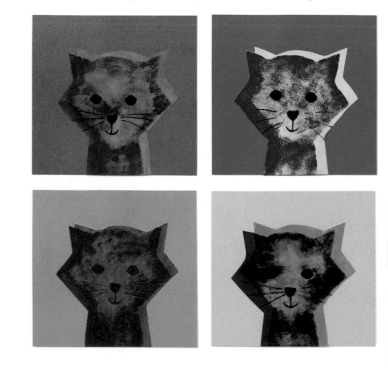

RAINY RACEHORSE

Degas learned to draw by copying.
Practice sketching from pictures of horses.
Then try out this pastel drawing
on blue textured paper.

 1 First draw the outline in pencil. If you want to copy
this horse, follow the shapes in the order below.
Draw it to one side of the page, like Degas did.

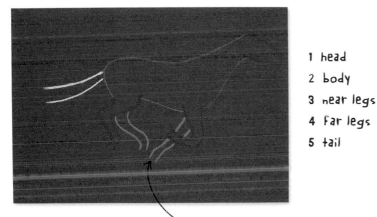

1 head
2 body
3 near legs
4 far legs
5 tail

— Don't worry about the feet!

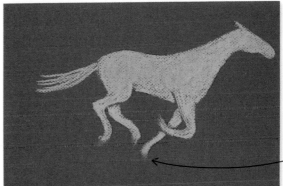 **2** Use a chalk pastel to color your horse. Smudge
with your finger to spread the color.

Smudge the
pastel at the
horse's feet.

 3 Choose a darker pastel to draw shadows on
the underside of the horse. Add highlights
to the upper areas with a lighter color.

— Draw an
eye and a
flowing
mane.

You can blend two
colors by smudging
them gently.

Let some rain go over the horse.

Do thick and thin
streaks of rain.

Make diagonal flicks
near the horse's feet.

4 Use marks like these
to draw some green
grass and then a rainy
blue-gray sky.

Make downward
streaks with the tip
of a pastel.

PLACES

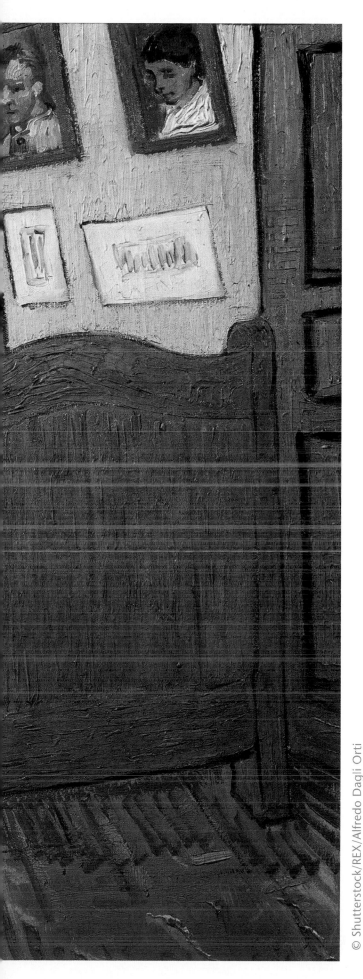

BEDROOM IN ARLES

Vincent van Gogh 1889

If you were to make a list of places where you spend a lot of time, your bedroom would probably be one of them. Van Gogh decided to paint a picture of his—three times!

Restful room

Van Gogh's room is very neat! He wanted us to feel restful when we look at it. There's a big comfy bed and sunlight streaming through the window; the colors are warm and bright. We see the artist's smocks hanging up, and the blue pitcher and bowl he used for washing. It's a calm, simple scene . . . but can you spot anything unusual?

Look at the doors—they're both blocked by furniture. The pictures make the wall seem to lean in, and the floor slopes down toward us. Van Gogh has used thick, chunky brushstrokes and bold outlines instead of shadows. All of these things stop the scene from being too ordinary!

WHO WAS VAN GOGH?

Vincent van Gogh was born in the Netherlands in 1853. He began painting in his famous colorful style after a move to France in the 1880s, but he struggled to sell his work. Poor and mentally ill, Van Gogh died at age 37. In ten years he had made an impressive 900 paintings! They sell for millions today.

GRAND CANAL
WITH SAN SIMEONE PICCOLO

Canaletto, *about* 1740

Imagine rowing a boat into the distance of this scene —it looks like a long way!
Of course it's just a flat painting, but Canaletto has managed to create an amazing sense of space.

A place to remember

Do you recognize this place? It's Venice, the famous Italian city. In the days before photography, tourists liked to take home paintings or drawings to remind them of their stay there. Canaletto was popular for his many detailed views, or *vedute*, of the city.

In this wide-angle picture, our eye travels from the busy foreground boats, past beautiful buildings, all the way to the distant canal bend. Canaletto draws us in using his skill at perspective, where things look smaller as they get farther away. He was excellent at capturing light and reflections on the water. One person said he could make the Sun shine in his work!

WHO WAS CANALETTO?

Giovanni Antonio Canal was born in Venice in 1697. He was nicknamed Canaletto ("little Canal") because his father was an artist, too. Both men worked as theater scenery painters, but Canaletto later switched to painting large canvases showing daily life in Venice and England.

LANDSCAPE AT CERET

Juan Gris 1913

No one has cut up this picture, but it looks a little like a jigsaw puzzle! Gris wanted to show a landscape in several ways at once, so he painted it in patchwork pieces.

Hotchpotch world

Look at the buildings in the middle. There are tiled rooftops seen from above, walls shown from the side, and some walls even upsidedown! The trees and hills are juggled around so that we see them from different viewpoints. It seems to be daytime with the bright, sunny colors—but there are hints of night darkness, too. It's like a jumble of memories of a place!

Gris was a Cubist like Gleizes (see p14). He loved to play around with space and shapes. He didn't want to trick people by making his work look three dimensional when paintings are actually flat!

If you compare this picture with the one on page 86, you'll see it looks much flatter. Gris and the Cubists thought that painting in perspective was far too limited! They wanted to show the world from many angles, not just a single viewpoint. This break from tradition shocked people at the time.

WHO WAS GRIS?

Juan Gris was born in Spain in 1887 but spent most of his working life in France. He was inspired by the leading Cubists, Pablo Picasso and Georges Braque. The world around them was changing, and photography was starting to replace realistic art. Cubism became a modern way of painting!

CASTLE AND SUN

Paul Klee 1928

This castle doesn't look as if it would stand for thousands of years—but it makes an impressive picture! Klee has built it up from many multicolored blocks, like a mosaic.

Rainbow walls

Klee was clever with color. The way he arranged the blocks makes us feel like we're looking at a castle, even though there's no real outline. We can pick out bright battlements, turrets, an archway, and the Sun, which zing out against darker areas. The design makes our eyes dart around the page!

Klee loved playing with geometric shapes to create magical designs and patterns. He often worked on several very different canvases at once. This painting is almost abstract, because you can't immediately tell what it is. The warm, cheerful colors and jostling shapes seem to take on a life of their own!

WHO WAS KLEE?

Paul Klee was born in Switzerland in 1879. As a boy he was good at music, but he soon discovered a talent for drawing, too. After a trip to Tunisia, he fell in love with color, which became the main focus of his painting. By the time he died in 1940, he had more than 9,000 works to his name!

MOUNT FUJI
IN CLEAR WEATHER

Katsushika Hokusai, about 1831

Could you draw the same place again and again? Hokusai loved Mount Fuji so much that he designed more than 140 different prints of it! This one comes from a series of 36 views.

Varied views

Hokusai's prints show Mount Fuji from the north, south, east, west . . . close up and far away. In this one, the snow-drizzled cone of the volcano glows red under a scattering of clouds. Notice how the trees look like specks on its giant slopes. The sky is printed in Prussian blue—a color that was new to Japan at the time. It helped make 36 Views of Mount Fuji a smash hit!

Hokusai used a printing technique called *ukiyo-e*. He would make a drawing, and then an assistant would glue it face down on a block of wood and cut away the blank areas. The block was inked and pressed onto paper, and then more blocks were made to print each color of the scene.

WHO WAS HOKUSAI?

Katsushika Hokusai was born in 1760 in Japan. He wasn't called Hokusai then—he changed his name many times throughout his life! Fascinated by drawing from the age of six, he enjoyed a long career as an artist. When he made his famous Mount Fuji prints, he was about 70 years old.

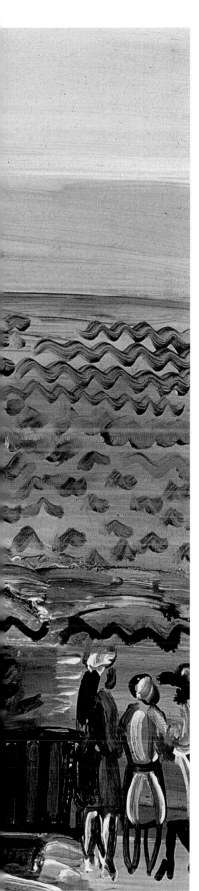

NIGHT AT SAINTE ADRESSE

Raoul Dufy, late 1920s–1930s

Do you love the beach?
We can tell Raoul Dufy did!

His painting conjures up a calm, contented feeling as the sun goes down over a rippling ocean.

Sketchy scene

Look at the people strolling along here—they are sketched in just a few lines. Dufy didn't worry about details like faces! We can see there are beach umbrellas as well as boats in the distance, but they're suggested by very simple marks. Instead of painting a realistic view, Dufy gives us an impression of the place.

Dufy's brushstrokes are thick and almost scribbly. They make everything seem to move. Bright reflections dance across the water and a warm, peachy glow fills the sky. Unlike traditional artists, who faded things into the distance to create a sense of space, Dufy painted vibrant colors all over his canvases!

WHO WAS DUFY?

Raoul Dufy was born in France in 1877. He grew up by the sea, along with his eight brothers and sisters. Dufy liked to paint the joyful things in life, from beach scenes to horseraces and sailing regattas. With his colorful, decorative style, he was also a successful fabric designer.

ABORIGINAL DOT PAINTING

Australian Aboriginal artist

This may not look like an obvious place, but that's what the artist intended! Australian Aboriginal dot paintings tell secret stories about the land and how the world was created.

Ancient art

Aboriginal peoples were the first to live in Australia. Their history and art traditions go back many thousands of years. This painting is a modern one, but it illustrates an ancient story in a way that only certain people can understand.

Every shape and pattern that we see here means something. The circles may be campsites, watering holes, or meeting places, while the U-shapes represent people. There are snakes, honey ants, and other symbols relating to the landscape and beliefs about it. Australian Aboriginal people have no written language, so paintings like this are a great way to pass down information through family lines.

Some Australian Aboriginal paintings reveal how to find a sacred site or watering hole, like magical maps that only those who know the land can read! Others illustrate stories from the dreamtime, when Australian Aboriginal people believe the world was created. Many paintings feature animals, animal tracks, plants, food, or the weather. Everything has its own symbol, which is read in a special way.

HOW WAS IT MADE?

Traditional Australian Aboriginal art takes many forms, from painting on rocks or bark to making pictures in the desert sand. Dot painting on canvas like this began in the 1970s. The artists use acrylic paints in earthy colors, such as browns, ochers, and greens. To make the dots, they dip in the end of a stick.

WINTER LANDSCAPE

Wassily Kandinsky 1909

What color is snow? You might say "white," but to Kandinsky it was all the colors of the rainbow! There's hardly any white at all in this painting of a wintry scene.

Cozy snow

Sometimes when you look at a snowy landscape, you can see hints of pink, blue, and yellow as sunlight shimmers across it. Kandinsky took this idea to extremes. He "turned up" the colors in his painting so that they are extra bold and bright. He laid them down in big, chunky brushstrokes.

Colors were very important to Kandinsky. He used them to show us not how his world looked, but how he felt about it. We know that snow is cold, but his pinks, oranges, and yellows warm it up like a cozy blanket! The little house glows invitingly against the cool blue shadows of a winter's day.

WHO WAS KANDINSKY?

Wassily Kandinsky was born in Russia in 1866. From a young age, he felt affected by colors and even said they made him hear different musical sounds. Eventually, Kandinsky's paintings became more about color than about recognizable subjects. He was one of the first artists to develop abstract art.

COMING OUT OF SCHOOL

L. S. Lowry 1927

Next time you're out, look around you. Notice people going about their daily lives. Lowry did this all the time! Then he went home and painted what he remembered.

Dreary day

It looks like a chilly day outside this school. Lowry has used dull grays, browns, and blues to show the dreary weather. He was good at capturing moods in this way, only ever using five paint colors. He would daub them on thickly, straight from the tube, blending and scraping with his fingers, a knife, or the end of his brush.

The people in this painting don't have a famous story. It's just like a glimpse of a moment in time. Lowry painted ordinary, everyday life in the factory towns of northern England. He became known for his scuttling "matchstick" figures—someone even wrote a song about them!

WHO WAS LOWRY?

Laurence Stephen Lowry was born in England in 1887. He spent his adult life working as a rent collector, painting and studying life drawing in his spare time. By the 1950s, his work was very popular, even with Queen Elizabeth! In 1967, *Coming Out of School* was printed on a postage stamp.

NEW YORK
UNDER GASLIGHT

Stuart Davis 1941

There's so much to look at in this painting that it's hard to know where to rest your eyes!

Davis has put together a mass of familiar shapes to create the feel of a busy city.

City snapshot

Imagine that you're rushing down a street—you catch glimpses of store windows, buildings, signs, and other things. That's what Davis shows us. We see a barbershop, a cigar store, skyscrapers, an overhead canopy, a statue, a flag, and a bridge. There are bricks and lettering. Nothing is complete, as if we're just passing quickly by.

Is it day or night in the picture? We can tell from the blazing gas lamp and the Moon. The sky is a dusky green, which sits back while the reds, whites, and yellows leap toward us. Davis knew that placing bright colors next to duller ones would create the illusion of 3D space— even though his shapes were completely flat!

WHO WAS DAVIS?

Stuart Davis was born in Pennsylvania in 1892. When he took up art, his teacher encouraged him to use daily life as his subject. He loved painting modern city sights such as electric signs and advertisements, and he often included words in his scenes. The lively sounds of jazz music also influenced his work.

THE HUMAN CONDITION

René Magritte 1933

At first this looks like a country scene through a window—then you realize it's a painting of that very scene, too! Magritte loved to make us look twice at his pictures.

A view—or two?

Can you see the easel and the edge of the canvas in the window? Magritte has covered part of his painting of a view with a painting of a painting that exactly matches it! If that makes you scratch your head, it's supposed to. It Is a kind of optical illusion—a trick of the eye.

Magritte liked the idea that the tree was both inside the room in the painting and outside in the "real" landscape. He thought it was similar to the way we see the world. For example, when we look at a chair, the picture we have in our head is the same as the chair, but it isn't the actual chair!

Magritte's style is called Surrealist, which basically means "beyond real." He painted ordinary objects but made us look at them in unusual ways. Because he was so skilled as a painter, he was able to play tricks on the viewer. Many of his pictures look real but impossible at the same time!

WHO WAS MAGRITTE?

René Magritte was born in Belgium in 1898. After studying art, he designed wallpaper and posters to earn money while he painted in his spare time. In 1927, he moved to Paris, France, but after a few years, he quarreled with other Surrealists and went home! Still, he continued painting in his own Surrealist style.

PROJECT CHECKLIST 3

These are the materials you'll need for each project in the Places section.
The ones in parentheses are useful, but you can manage without them!

Brush a bedroom (page 107)
thick white paper, pencil, eraser, paper plate or palette, acrylic paints,
school glue, paintbrushes, (toothpick, fork)

In perspective (page 108)
white paper, pencil, eraser, ruler, colored pencils or pens, scissors

Slice a scene (page 109)
thick white paper, pencil, eraser, ruler, acrylic or tempera paints,
paintbrushes, scissors, glue, large piece of colored paper

Castle and Moon (page 110)
2 large sheets of colored paper (one light, one dark), pencil,
eraser, brightly colored papers, scissors, glue

Mount Splatter (page 111)
sponge cloths, scissors, glue, stiff cardboard, acrylic paints,
paintbrushes, colored paper, drinking straw

Sunset strips (page 112)
thick white paper, pencil, eraser, tissue paper, glue, oil pastels or crayons

Dreamy designs (page 113)
colored paper, pencil, rubber, acrylic or tempera paints, paintbrush, paper plate

Rainbow snow (page 114)
colored pastel paper, pencil, eraser, soft pastels

Stand-up city (page 115)
cardboard, pencil, scissors, magazines or scrap paper, glue, dark paper

City lights (page 116)
large black paper or posterboard, other colored papers, including orange, scissors,
glue, eraser (or sponge or potato), acrylic paint, paintbrush, paper plate or palette,
cardboard, bottle cap, pencil (or Bubble Wrap)

Outside-in (page 117)
pale blue posterboard, white acrylic, tempera paint, cotton ball, green posterboard,
pencil, eraser, scissors, glue, different colored posterboard, (brown acrylic paint)

BRUSH A BEDROOM

Paint your own bedroom **in chunky brushstrokes like Van Gogh!**

1 On a piece of thick paper, draw the outline of your room. Don't worry about getting it exactly right—if it's a little topsy-turvy, it will be more like Van Gogh's!

Straighten up first so you don't have to paint too many small and cluttered things!

2 On a paper plate, mix acrylic paint with some school glue to thicken it. Paint the larger areas first, laying the color on thickly with a wide brush.

Don't try to go right to the edges— you can fill in the gaps at the end.

3 While the paint is still wet, scrape patterns into it with a toothpick, fork, or the end of your brush.

You can swirl two colors together if you like!

4 Continue painting and scraping different textures. Finally, fill in any gaps using a fine brush.

If you want to add extra details, wait for the paint to dry first.

Follow these steps to draw a row of houses and trees

IN PERSPECTIVE

1 With a ruler and pencil, draw a line straight across the page. This is the horizon (h). Mark a point along the line. This is the vanishing point (v). Draw diagonal lines from the vanishing point to the edges of the page, as shown.

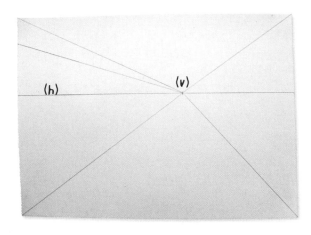

2 For the houses, draw the vertical lines (a) first. Follow the diagonal lines to draw walls going away from you (b). For the side walls, draw lines straight across (c).

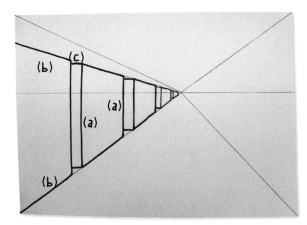

3 Use the top diagonal line to draw the roofs. You can add chimneys if you like. On the opposite side of the page, draw a row of trees between the diagonal lines.

Draw lines for the sidewalk and grass, both meeting at the vanishing point. The space between them will be the road.

4 Draw in the detail. Use a ruler to help make sure all lines going away from you lead to the vanishing point.

Cut out a figure and place it on the page. What happens if you move it into the distance?

SLICE A SCENE

Mix and match night and day **in this Cubist chop-up painting!**

1 Draw a line down the middle of a piece of thick white paper. One side will be night; the other day. Sketch a landscape across the page using simple lines and shapes.

Make some house and tree shapes big and closeup, and others small and distant.

2 Now you can paint the scene. Do a bright sky and sunny colors on one side, and a dark sky and dimmer colors on the other.

You don't have to be too neat—let your brushstrokes show!

3 When your finished painting is dry, cut it into strips. Make some strips wider than others—it doesn't matter if your cutting goes a little crooked.

4 Jumble up your painted strips to create a new scene. Turn some of them upsidedown. Glue them onto a larger piece of colored paper, leaving a border like a frame around the edge.

Overlap some strips if you need to, or leave narrow gaps between a few of them!

CASTLE AND MOON

Choose nighttime colors **for this moonlit castle mosaic!**

1 You'll need two large sheets of paper—one light-colored and the other dark. On the light paper, sketch the outline of a castle and Moon.

Keep the drawing simple —it's just a guide!

3 When your castle is complete, cut it out. Leave a narrow border of the light-colored paper around the edge.

2 Cut out your mosaic pieces from different colored papers. Starting in one corner, arrange them like a puzzle to fill in the castle. Glue them down.

Leave a small gap between the pieces so that they look like tiles.

4 Stick your castle onto the dark sheet of paper. Cut out a bright Moon and glue it on.

You could add a couple more mosaic blocks at the sides.

MOUNT SPLATTER

You can recreate this erupting volcano **as many times as you like!**

1 To make a printing plate, cut out a volcano and smoke shapes from a sponge cloth. Stick them with craft glue onto cardboard—the back of an old sketchbook is good.

Add some shapes for land and water in the foreground.

2 When the glue is dry, cover the shapes thickly with acrylic paint. You can swirl two colors together for a streaky effect. While the paint is still wet, press it down firmly onto red paper.

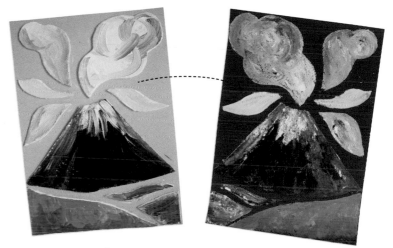

When you peel off the printing plate, the print underneath will be in reverse!

4 Wipe off any excess paint from the printing plate and let it dry a while. Then try printing and splattering with some different colors!

3 Let the paint dry before you erupt your volcano! Water down some red and yellow paint and drop a little onto the summit. Blow through a straw to make the paint trickle down the sides.

Lay down plenty of newspaper for this part!

Finish by splattering paint over the page by flicking a brush.

SUNSET STRIPS

Doodle like Dufy **on a tissue paper background!**

1 First sketch out your scene on a piece of thick white paper. Draw a line for the horizon, a sun, some boats, beach umbrellas, and people. Try to suggest the shapes in just a few lines!

Press down hard so that you can see the lines through tissue paper.

2 Now tear some strips of tissue paper. Glue them down, one at a time, to make a fiery sky. Stick a round, red Sun on top, and then start on the ocean.

You can layer light strips over dark to make different colors.

4 When the background is dry, go over your pencil lines with an oil pastel or crayon. Doodle quickly—you don't have to be too accurate!

3 To make sunny reflections, stick small pieces of orange, pink, and yellow tissue paper over the ocean.

You could add some wiggly lines for waves.

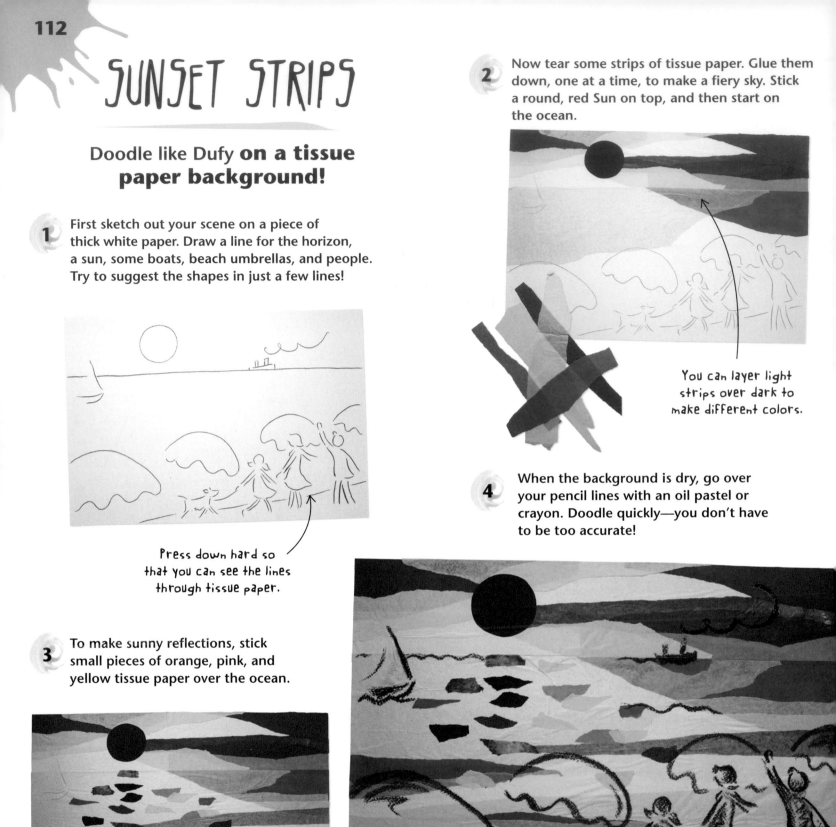

DREAMY DESIGNS

 Look online for patterns and symbols used in Australian Aboriginal art, **then have a go with this finger painting!**

1 Sketch the main shapes of your design on a piece of orange, yellow, or brown paper.

2 Using a paintbrush and dark-colored paint, fill in the lines and a few of the shapes.

3 Now squeeze some paint onto a paper plate or palette. Dip your fingertip into a color, and then press it onto the page. You can print a few dots before dipping into more paint. Print one color at a time!

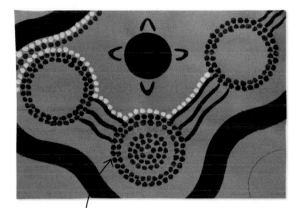

To fit within a circle, you might have to space some dots more than others.

4 Continue dipping and dotting until you've filled the whole page!

RAINBOW SNOW

See how colors make you feel **with these no-white snow scenes!**

1 Sketch out your scene on a piece of red or orange pastel paper. Using yellow chalk or a yellow pastel, start to color patches of it.

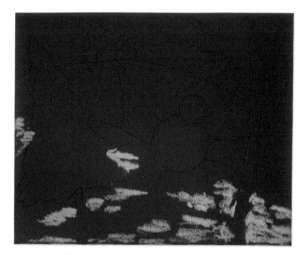

2 Add patches of other warm, light colors such as orange and pink. You can blend colors together using your finger, or let parts of the background show through.

Use softer, duller colors in the distance.

3 Add darker colors for trees and shadows last.

4 Try recreating your scene using cool colors such as pale blues and greens. See how different it feels!

Experiment with as many different colors as you like!

Very pale colors look almost white against the darker paper.

STAND-UP CITY

Make a 3D version of a Lowry scene!

1 On a tall piece of cardboard, draw some factory buildings and cut them out along the skyline. Cut window and door shapes from magazines or scrap paper and stick them on.

2 Make a row of houses in the same way, but not as tall as the factories. To make the buildings stand up, stick cardboard flaps to the back, as shown.

Fold strips of cardboard and glue them to the back at each side.

3 Fold a strip of dark paper back and forth like an accordian. Draw a figure on the top layer with the hands reaching to the sides. Cut it out.

Don't cut here.

Unfold your chain of people!

4 Now you can arrange your scene. Stand the houses in front of the factories and the people in front of them.

You could stick some colorful clothes on the people!

CITY LIGHTS

Use bright colors against dark ones **to create a lit-up city scene!**

1 For the background, use a large piece of black paper or posterboard. Cut a triangle of orange paper to suggest the glare of city lights and glue it on.

2 Now cut out some colorful skyscrapers, smaller buildings, and other simple shapes that remind you of a city. Arrange them on the background and glue them down.

You can stick a black building against the orange sky.

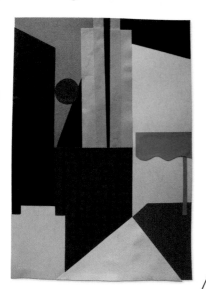

3 To print windows, cover the side or end of a rectangular eraser in acrylic paint and press it onto the buildings. Use different surfaces of the eraser to print different shapes.

You could print using pieces cut from a sponge or potato instead.

4 To print lines, paint the edge of a piece of cardboard and press it onto the page. For circular shapes, do the same with the rim of a bottle cap.

You can print lights with the end of a pencil or a strip of Bubble Wrap!

OUTSIDE-IN

Make people look twice **with these surreal scenes!**

1 On a piece of blue posterboard, paint some clouds. To do this, dip a cotton ball in white paint and dab it on in patches. Cover the page!

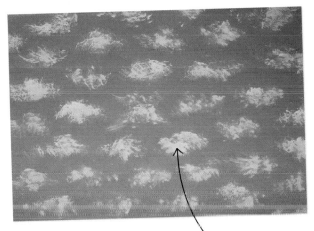

Dab more lightly in some places for a fluffy effect.

2 On half a piece of green posterboard, draw the shape of a tree. Carefully cut it out and keep both pieces.

Keep the tree shape simple.

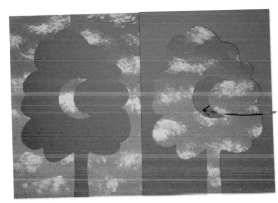

3 Lay the tree on one side of your cloud page and the outside piece on the other. Glue them down.

If you like, you could cut a moon shape from the leftover half of green posterboard and stick it on in the middle.

4 What other things can you turn outside-in in the same way? Here are a few ideas!

Cut out a car and make it fly . . .

. . . or create a city in the sky!

Print bricks by dipping the end of a rectangular eraser in brown paint.

STORIES

© Shutterstock/REX/Gianni Dagli Orti

WILLIAM THE CONQUEROR'S FLEET

Bayeux Tapestry 1000s

Imagine a cartoon strip that's three-fourths the size of a football field!

That's one way to describe the Bayeux Tapestry, which this sailing scene is a part of.

Sewn story

If you saw the whole Bayeux Tapestry, it might take you a while to find this boat—you'd have to search 230 feet (70 meters) of cloth decorated with 632 people, 202 horses, 560 other creatures, 41 ships, and a lot more! The pictures tell the story of William the Conqueror and his invasion of England more than 900 years ago.

This scene shows William's fleet crossing the English Channel from Normandy, France. They're on their way to victory at the Battle of Hastings. We can see the sails billowing on their wooden longboats, laden with horses, soldiers, and shields. Every tiny detail is sewn in woolen yarn on linen fabric. In fact, this type of stitching isn't called tapestry at all, but embroidery!

WHY WAS IT MADE?

The story on the Bayeux Tapestry is told from the invaders' point of view, so it was probably made as a celebration. We think that it was ordered by William's half brother, Bishop Odo of Bayeux. No one really knows who sewed it, but it might have been a group of nuns who were skilled at needlework.

HOMAGE TO BLÉRIOT

Robert Delaunay 1914

In 1909, an exciting story hit the news —someone had flown a plane across the English Channel! A few years later, Robert Delaunay celebrated it on canvas.

Soaring shapes

Flying a plane from France to England might not be a big deal today, but Louis Blériot was the first person to do it! He won a prize of £1,000 and became a hero on both sides of the English Channel. Delaunay chose a rainbow of flight-inspired shapes to honor him.

Look at the circles—do they remind you of spinning propellers? There's a biplane soaring above the Eiffel Tower, but Blériot flew a monoplane with only one set of wings. Can you see it here? Delaunay didn't want to create a detailed, realistic scene. Instead, he painted bright, simple shapes that seem to whirl and flicker. They make us feel the energy and thrill of flying through the air!

WHO WAS DELAUNAY?

Robert Delaunay was born in France in 1885. He worked as a theater designer before becoming a painter. As an artist he was inspired by different modern styles, from Impressionism to Cubism and Expressionism. He blended them in his own colorful world of bold, often abstract shapes.

SCENE FROM
CINDERELLA

Arthur Rackham 1919

You might recognize this scene from a folklore version of *Cinderella*. Rackham brings the famous story to life with his simple but magical illustrations.

Telling tails

Can you tell what's happening here? The fairy godmother is turning six lizards into footmen! We can see them changing little by little from animal to human—look at their tails getting shorter. They'll soon be ready to take Cinderella to the ball in her pumpkin carriage.

Of course, *Cinderella* is a made-up story, so no one really knows what the fairy godmother looked like. Rackham imagined her as a friendly, witchy character with a long nose and a pointy hat! He illustrated this scene and the rest of the book in a style called silhouette. He was excellent at showing poses and expressions through plain black shapes with very little detail within them.

WHO WAS RACKHAM?

Arthur Rackham was born in England in 1867. He grew up loving to draw, and later made his name as a great illustrator. Known for his imaginative characters and enchanted scenes, he decorated the pages of many famous books—from children's fairy tales to plays by William Shakespeare!

AUTOMAT

Edward Hopper 1927

Some stories are imagined—and some make us do the imagining! In this painting, Hopper sets the scene for a story but leaves a sense of mystery dangling over it.

Puzzling picture

The painting makes us ask a lot of questions. Who is this woman? What is she doing here? Is she waiting for someone? What kind of mood is she in? She is well dressed and wearing makeup. Is she on her way to or from work or a party? Her clothes suggest that it's cold outside, but we can't tell from the dark sky whether it is early morning or night.

How long do you think the woman has been here? She's still wearing a glove, so perhaps she has only recently sat down. But we can also see an empty plate in front of her—has she had time for something to eat? Maybe she is thinking about leaving. There's no action to give away the full story. Hopper leaves it up to us to fill in the gaps!

WHO WAS HOPPER?

Edward Hopper was born in New York in 1882. He studied art and worked briefly as an illustrator before making his name as a painter. Hopper became famous for his quiet city scenes with isolated figures and dramatic lighting. Most of the women that he painted were modeled on his wife.

NOAH'S ARK

Canterbury Cathedral 1200s

Windows aren't just for looking out of—sometimes they tell stories instead! This one, made of colorful stained glass, illustrates a scene from the Bible.

Seeing the light

The man we can see here is Noah. In the Bible story, he builds a giant ark to save his family and two of every type of animal from a terrible flood. One day he sends out a dove, which returns with an olive branch in its beak. This tells Noah that the flood is easing off and land is somewhere within reach.

Imagine this picture as part of a huge cathedral window packed with religious scenes. It was made at a time when few people were able to read, but they could learn a lot from the bright stained-glass images. As the sun moved around throughout the day, different windows would come alive like a colored light show. It must have been exciting long before movies or television were invented!

Stained glass is still used as an art form to tell stories, celebrate people's lives or events, or just decorate rooms with dancing patterns of light. You can see windows like this in churches, mosques, synagogues, and many other buildings—some people even have them in their homes! The way stained glass is made has barely changed since it was invented, though many more colors are available today.

HOW WAS IT MADE?

The glass had to be melted and colored with chemicals before cooling and flattening out. Small details, such as faces and feathers, were painted on—often with a black pigment mixed with urine! The pieces were carefully cut to shape and then arranged and joined together with strips of lead.

THE SPINNERS

Diego Velázquez, *about* 1657

This large painting tells a story in two parts. It begins in the foreground, close to the viewer, and then continues at the back of the scene.

Weaving a tale

Velázquez chose a Greek myth, the fable of Arachne, as the subject of his painting. It tells of a peasant girl named Arachne who challenged the goddess Athena to a weaving contest. When Arachne produced a tapestry as beautiful as Athena's, the goddess became angry—and turned the poor girl into a spider!

Athena is the figure in the headscarf, while Arachne has her back to us on the right. They are busy spinning yarn for their work. Velázquez arranged them carefully, leading our eye slowly toward the lit-up back room where Arachne's finished tapestry hangs on the wall. We can see Athena in a helmet in front of it, raising her arm in fury. Velázquez expects us to know what happens next!

WHO WAS VELÁZQUEZ?

Diego Velázquez was born in Spain in 1599. At the age of 11, he became apprenticed to a local painter who recognized his artistic talent. Later he was made court painter to King Philip IV and lived in the royal palace. He also traveled to Italy, where other great artists influenced his work.

LONE DOG'S WINTER COUNT

Lone Dog 1800–1870

Here's a story that you read from the inside out!

Each symbol in this spiral represents a year in the life of the Native American Yanktonai Nakota people.

Dates to remember

We may use dates in our diaries, but Lone Dog and others used pictures instead. Every year, they chose the most memorable thing that had happened and drew a symbol, or pictograph, for it. This built up a decorative record of their history—there are 70 years shown here.

Try to find the following: a spotted figure (many people died of smallpox), a lasso (wild horses were caught), two hands about to shake (a peace agreement), a black Sun (solar eclipse). Other events include trading with Europeans, battles with other tribes, floods, pony thefts, and a meteor shower. They're all drawn on a buffalo skin, or hide.

WHY A WINTER COUNT?

It's called a winter count because the Nakota measured their years between each first snowfall. Every year, the elders met to decide on the event to record. As time passed, the keeper of the count had to remember what his symbols meant so that he could tell the stories to others!

THE ARMADA PORTRAIT

Probably George Gower, *about* 1588

Every person has a story—and Elizabeth I of England's was an impressive one! This painting is more than just a portrait of the powerful and popular queen.

Glory story

In the year that this picture was painted, the English defeated an invasion from Spain known as the Spanish Armada. We can see two scenes from the battle in the background, on each side of the queen. Under her hand is a globe, a symbol of the power that she held in the world. Her clothes and jewels tell us that she was rich and grand.

In fact, this visual story has a few fibs in it, too. In 1588, Elizabeth was 55 years old, with rotting teeth and probably some wrinkles! This wasn't the image she wanted people to remember, so the artist painted her as an ageless beauty surrounded by wealth and glory.

WHO WAS GOWER?

This picture isn't signed by George Gower, but it seems likely that he painted it. Born in England around 1540, he became "serjeant painter" to Queen Elizabeth in 1581. His main job was to create portraits of the royals, but he also painted decorations on their furniture, palaces, and carriages.

WORLD UPSIDE DOWN

Jan Steen, *about* 1665

The world isn't actually upside down in this painting—but it isn't quite how it should be. Steen has woven in all sorts of little stories that tip ordinary life on its head!

Rowdy room

What do you see when you look at this household? Is there anything that seems a little strange? Maybe it's the boy smoking a pipe, the lady asleep at the table, or the dog devouring her dinner! No one seems to notice the baby throwing her food and playing with an expensive necklace. There's an indoor pig, a duck on a guest, and a monkey playing with a clock!

Jan Steen had a sense of humor. He loved to make jokes about the ordered lifestyles of people in the villages around him. While other Dutch artists painted prim and proper families in well-kept homes, Steen showed children with grownup bad habits and adults goofing off like kids!

WHO WAS STEEN?

Jan Steen was born in Holland in 1625 or 1626. He came from a family of brewers, and his paintings told stories of the everyday life around him. Often he included witty proverbs, or messages, in his work. World Upside Down is also known as Beware of Luxury—a warning about the penalties of being rich!

THE BATTLE
OF SAN ROMANO

Paolo Uccello, *about* 1438–1440

The good thing about painting a battle story is you can pick the parts you show! Uccello chose glory over gory in this enormous picture, painted for a family on the winning side.

A beautiful battle

In real life, Uccello's painting is 10 feet (3 meters) wide! It tells the story of a battle between the Italian cities of Florence and Sienna. Can you guess who is leading the victorious Florentine side? Of course it's the man on the white horse! He's Niccolò da Tolentino, and he's the first thing we notice in the scene.

Uccello has ignored a lot of the reality of battle. His hero doesn't even wear a helmet to protect his head. Instead, we see decorative costumes, beautiful scenery, and a crisscross pattern of scattered swords. Uccello had just discovered the technique of perspective, which gave his painting a 3D feel. Apparently, he would stay up all night trying to get the angles exactly right!

WHO WAS UCCELLO?

Paolo di Dono was born in Italy in 1397. ("Uccello" was really a nickname, given for his love of painting birds.) He became apprenticed to a sculptor at the age of ten, and then turned to painting in his teens. This picture, one of three that he made of the same battle, is one of his most famous works.

DREAM OF A SUNDAY AFTERNOON IN ALAMEDA CENTRAL PARK

Diego Rivera 1947

Sometimes the strangest stories happen in our dreams! In this dreamlike painting, Rivera takes a walk in the park with hundreds of characters from history.

Distant memories

The boy in striped socks is the artist himself, aged ten, with a frog and snake in his pockets. He holds hands with a living skeleton woman dressed in a fancy plumed hat. Skeleton characters were a speciality of the artist José Guadalupe Posada, who stands on her other side. Behind the young Rivera we can also see Frida Kahlo, his future wife.

This is just a section of Rivera's huge picture, which he painted on a hotel wall. He mixed his own memories with the story of his home country, Mexico. While some scenes seem like the stuff of nightmares, the hot-air balloon is a symbol of hope. It's decorated with the colors of the Mexican flag and "RM" for *República Mexicana*.

WHO WAS RIVERA?

Diego Rivera was born in Mexico in 1886. Even as a boy he loved drawing on walls, so no wonder he became famous for his murals! Rivera liked to paint scenes with messages that often shocked other people. He created huge public pictures so that everyone could see what he believed in.

PROJECT CHECKLIST 4

Below is a list of materials that you'll need for each project in the Stories section.
The ones in parentheses are useful, but you can manage without them!

Sew a boat (page 143)
colorful felt or other strong fabric, scissors, different colored yarn,
large needle, glue

Salute to space (page 144)
thick white paper, pencil, eraser, round objects or compass,
oil pastels or crayons, watercolor paint, paintbrush, (cloth)

Character cutouts (page 145)
scrap paper, pen or pencil, scissors, black paper, white pencil,
glue, white paper, (colored paper)

Secret story (page 146)
colored pastel paper, pencil, eraser, soft pastels

Window wings (page 147)
letter-size or larger black paper, white pencil or crayon, scissors,
colored tissue paper, glue, adhesive putty

Spinning spiders (page 148)
stiff cardboard, pen or pencil, thick string or cord, scissors, strong craft glue,
white paint, paper plate, colored paper, black paint, black felt-tip pen or marker

What counts? (page 149)
thick white paper, tea bags, pencil, felt-tip pens, crayons or paints and paintbrush

Dressing up (page 150)
colored paper, scissors, glue, paints, paper plate or palette, pencil, pen lid or bottle cap,
leaves, strip of cardboard, potato, onion or cabbage, tinfoil, (gems or sequins)

Silly street (page 151)
drawing paper or posterboard, pencil, eraser, colored paper,
scissors, glue, old magazines, scraps of patterned paper

Battle in a box (page 152)
large shoebox, paper, scissors, paints, paintbrush, glue, thin cardboard,
(yarn, feathers, drinking straws, shiny paper)

Up and away! (page 153)
air-dry modeling clay, paintbrush, pencil, acrylic or tempera paints,
string, scissors

SEW A BOAT

Follow these steps **to stitch your own sailing scene!**

1 Using colorful felt or other strong fabric, cut out the shape of a boat and sail.

2 Thread a large needle with colored yarn and knot the end. On a spare piece of fabric, practice making stitches like these. If you haven't sewn before, ask an adult to help you.

This straight stitch is also called a running stitch.

Sew a row of running stitches, and then weave another color through the stitches.

Make a row of up-and-down stitches.

Sew diagonals to make Xs.

3 Use the stitches that you've learned to decorate the boat and sail with different colored yarn.

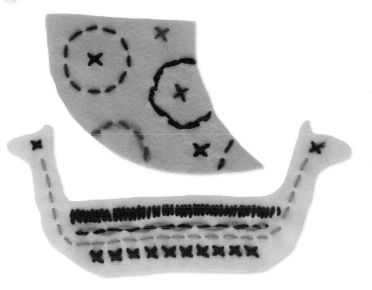

4 Stitch or glue your boat and sail onto another piece of fabric. Sew a mast and some wiggly lines for waves.

You could sew on some sailors, too.

Why not make a series of scenes and line them up like a cartoon strip!

SALUTE TO SPACE

Use Delaunay's colorful style **to make a tribute to modern space flight!**

1 On a piece of thick white paper, draw some space-inspired shapes. Think of swirling galaxies, planets, stars, moons, rockets, or even satellites—keep them simple!

Draw around circular objects, or use a compass.

2 Color in your shapes using oil pastels or crayons. The harder you press, the bolder the colors will be.

You can smudge colors together with your finger or a cloth.

3 Keep coloring until you've filled in the main shapes—leave the background blank.

4 Brush dark blue or black watercolor paint all over the background and any other gaps. The colored areas will resist the paint!

CHARACTER CUTOUTS

Choose a scene from your favorite fairy tale **and illustrate it with a silhouette!**

1 First practice drawing your characters on scrap paper. Show them from a side view, with the nose and arms sticking out. Just draw the outline —you won't see anything else in a silhouette.

Think about their mood and what they're doing —a pose can say a lot.

You can exaggerate noses, chins, and hair for funny characters!

2 When you're happy with a character, cut it out and place it face down on black paper. Draw around it in white pencil and cut it out.

Turn the cutout over so that you can't see any white lines.

3 Repeat step 2 for the other figures and features in your scene.

Include a couple of color details if you like!

4 Now arrange your cutouts on white paper or cardboard and glue them down. You could make a decorative border to finish off the picture!

Fold a strip of black paper back and forth like an accordion. Cut small shapes into the folds, and then open the paper out.

SECRET STORY

Think up your own story to illustrate in a mysterious scene!

1 On a piece of colored pastel paper, sketch out a scene. Include a person, a light of some kind, and small details that make the viewer ask questions.

2 Using a bright yellow or white soft pastel, color the areas where the light is coming from.

3 Gradually color in the rest of the scene using colored pastels. You can blend colors together using your fingers.

End of a pastel

Side of a pastel

Two colors blended with a finger

4 Finish with strong, bright highlights and dark shadows. Then ask a friend to guess what's happening in your story!

Lighten the places that the light would be shining on.

Shadows fall away from the light.

WINDOW WINGS

You can create the effect of stained glass **with some black paper and colored tissue paper.**

1 Fold a piece of letter-size (or larger) black paper in half. On one side, draw half of a butterfly using a white pencil or crayon. Cut it out, keeping the fold.

Folded edge is here.

2 With the paper still folded, draw on some simple shapes for markings. Leave a gap between them and around the edge. Carefully cut out the shapes.

Pinch the paper in the middle of a shape and cut a small slit. Then cut around the shape from the inside.

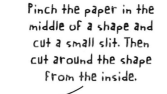

Now open out your butterfly.

3 Lay your butterfly pencil side up. Cut pieces of tissue paper a little bigger than the holes. Glue around the edges of the holes and stick the tissue paper down.

Do matching colors on each side.

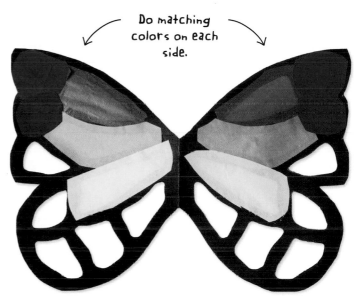

4 Turn your butterfly over and stick it to a window using adhesive putty. If you make another butterfly, they can fly to Noah's Ark two by two!

SPINNING SPIDERS

Create the next scene in Arachne's story **by showing her as a spider spinning webs!**

1 On a piece of stiff cardboard, draw a spider web. Keep it simple—too many lines will make it difficult to print.

Draw the diagonal lines first.

2 Starting with the diagonals again, cut pieces of thick string or cord to the length of the lines. Cover each line with strong craft glue and stick the string down.

3 When the glue is dry, squeeze some white paint onto a paper plate. Use a sponge to cover the web in paint, and then press it firmly down onto a sheet of colored paper.

When you lift off the cardboard, you'll find a print!

4 Take a large piece of colored paper and print several webs by repeating step 3. Then dip your thumb in black paint to print some spiders. Paint on eyes and draw the legs with a felt-tip pen or marker.

You can print extra lines using the edge of a piece of cardboard.

WHAT COUNTS?

Illustrate your own life story **in the style of a winter count!**

1 First prepare your background. Scrunch up a big piece of thick white paper, and then open it out again. Soak a few black tea bags in warm water and squeeze and dab them over the paper. Leave to dry.

The more tea you use, the darker the effect will be.

2 Now write a list of things that you remember from different times in your life. Think of at least 20 if you can. For each one, design your own special symbol. Here are a few examples:

Think about birthdays, family events, vacations, school field trips, and other activities.

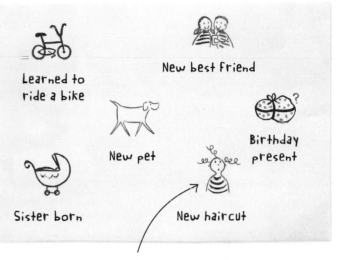

Learned to ride a bike

New best friend

New pet

Birthday present

Sister born

New haircut

Make the symbols as simple or as colorful as you like!

3 Tear a rough edge around the paper to make it look like a buffalo hide. Then draw or paint your symbols in the order that they happened.

Start in the middle and work in a spiral, turning the paper as you go.

If you leave some space, you can keep adding to your life-story picture!

Day at the movies

Great party!

Getting into art!

Long trip

DRESSING UP

Imagine you're part of a royal family—**design yourself a costume as grand as Elizabeth I's!**

Print your own "fabrics" by painting different objects and then pressing them onto paper.

Princess dress

End of a pencil

Pieces of a cupcake case or doily make great collars and cuffs!

Leaf

Rim of a pen lid or bottle cap

Edge of a strip of cardboard

Royal robe

Print with half an onion or a section of cabbage.

Scrape patterns into wet acrylic paint.

Prince's pajamas

Cut triangle or rectangle shapes from a potato and use them to print patterns.

Roll up a narrow strip of paper for a button.

Twist pieces of tinfoil into decorative shapes.

Crown

Try sticking on gems or sequins. **You could draw or paint a picture of yourself in the costume—and add things in the background that say a little about you and your hobbies!**

SILLY STREET

Turn the world upside down, inside out, and topsy-turvy **in this fun collage!**

1 Think of an ordinary, everyday setting such as a street, room, or school playground. Make a sketch of it, but fill it with a lot of strange or funny details.

Clothes standing on the line?

It's raining upward!

Hat feathers for a nest!

Where are his shoes?

Look out—there's a hole!

2 Use a large piece of paper or posterboard for your collage. Start by cutting out and sticking down the main background features, as shown.

Weird—the sky's green!

Cut face shapes from skin-colored paper and hairstyles from hair photos.

3 Look around for old magazines and scraps of patterned paper. Cut out shapes for the details in your picture and glue them down. Work from the background forward.

Try pictures of fur, wool, or carpet for animals and pictures of feathers for birds.

See if a friend can spot all of the things that are wrong!

BATTLE IN A BOX

Play with space like Uccello and create a 3D scene, or diorama, in a box!

1 You'll need a large shoebox or something similar. Cut a piece of paper the same size as the box base and paint or stick on a simple landscape. Glue it inside the box.

You could decorate the sides of the box, too.

2 Practice sketching a rearing horse and rider, and then draw it onto thin cardboard. Then cut out the shape, leaving some extra cardboard at the bottom to make a flap.

Use these red lines as a guide for drawing the horse.

Draw a rock behind the back legs so you don't have to cut them out.

3 Turn your horse face down on some more cardboard, draw around it, and cut it out. Paint or decorate the figures, facing opposite ways. Fold back the flaps to make them stand.

Try sticking on yarn for reins, a feather on a helmet, and spears cut from drinking straws or cardboard.

4 Make as many horsemen as you like. Then arrange your battle scene in the box!

Why not cut out some swords and shields to scatter on the ground.

UP AND AWAY!

Rivera made his paintings on fresh plaster. **You can create a similar effect on modeling clay.**

1 Roll out a block of air-dry modeling clay until it's about half an inch (1.25 cm) thick. Use the end of a paintbrush to pierce two holes right through the clay near the top. Let it dry overnight.

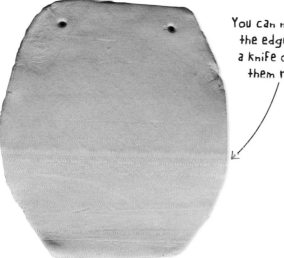

You can neaten up the edges with a knife or leave them rough.

2 Now think up a story based on a hot-air balloon—it could be a little wacky, like a dream! Where is it going? Who's onboard? When your clay is dry, draw on a scene in pencil.

No one will get their hands on this flying pirate's treasure!

4 Thread a piece of string through the holes and knot the ends together at the back. You can now hang your picture on a wall!

3 When you're happy with your outline, use acrylic or tempera paints to color it in. Let the painting dry.

ART WORDS AND INFO

abstract Not representing an actual object, place, or living thing. Abstract art often focuses on simplified shapes, lines, colors, or use of space.

anatomy The way a living thing is built. In humans this includes bones, muscles, and other inside parts.

apprentice Someone who works for an employer in order to learn a certain skill.

auction A sale where people bid for items and the bidder offering the highest price wins.

canvas A strong type of fabric on which artists can paint or sew designs.

carve To shape something by cutting into it. An artist may carve wood, stone, or other materials to make a sculpture.

collage A picture made by sticking pieces of paper, fabric, or other objects onto a surface.

commission To pay someone to create a particular item, such as a portrait.

complementary (or contrasting) colors Colors that are opposite each other on the color wheel (see panel below). If you place contrasting colors next to each other, they stand out more.

court painter An artist who painted for a royal or noble family, often agreeing not to take on other work.

Cubism (1907–1920s) An art style in which artists, including Juan Gris and Albert Gleizes, made images using simplified geometric shapes and multiple viewpoints.

easel A wooden stand that supports an artist's canvas or drawing board.

COLOR CONNECTIONS

In art there are three primary colors—**red**, **yellow**, and **blue**. These are colors that can't be mixed from any others. Each primary color has an opposite color, or complementary color, which is made by mixing the other two primary colors.

If you mix a color with its complementary color, you'll get a shade of brown.

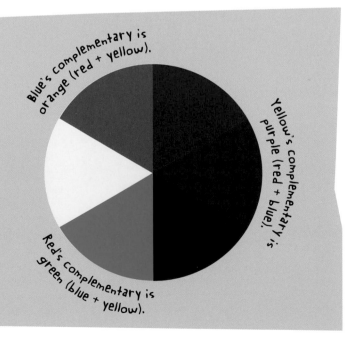

Blue's complementary is orange (red + yellow).

Yellow's complementary is purple (red + blue).

Red's complementary is green (blue + yellow).

embroidery The art of decorating fabric with stitched designs in yarn or thread.

engrave To scratch an image into a hard surface. Prints can be made from designs or lettering engraved on metal sheets.

exhibit To display work for people to see—for example, in a gallery or museum.

Expressionism (1905–1920s) An art style that was all about feelings and emotions, often shown through exaggerated colors or shapes. Edvard Munch, Franz Marc, and Wassily Kandinsky all worked in the Expressionist style.

Fauvism (about 1905–1910) An art style that focused on strong, vibrant colors and bold brushstrokes.

geometric shape A recognized mathematical shape, such as a triangle.

gold leaf Gold that is beaten out into very thin, delicate sheets and used for decoration.

horizon The line, as far away as we can see, where the land or ocean seems to meet the sky.

idealized Shown in an ideal or unnaturally perfect form.

illusion Something that seems to be one thing when it's actually another.

illustration A picture that explains or decorates a story or other piece of writing.

illustrator An artist who creates illustrations.

imperial Relating to an empire or its royal rulers, called emperors.

impression An idea or feeling about something.

Impressionism (1870s–1890s) An art style that focused on color and the changing effects of light. Impressionist artists often painted outdoors and tried to capture passing moments. Edgar Degas was an Impressionist.

landscape A scene or painting of a scene, usually in the countryside.

life drawing Drawing a human figure, often a model in an art class.

linoleum A tough, washable material with a smooth surface. Artists can scrape a design into it and then cover it with paint or ink to make a print.

lithograph A type of print in which the design is drawn onto stone or metal with a greasy substance. This is then covered with ink, which clings only to the greasy areas, and printed onto paper.

mosaic A design made up of small pieces of glass, tile, or other material, stuck onto a surface.

mural A picture painted on a wall.

mythological Relating to myths—traditional stories told by ancient cultures such as the ancient Greeks.

ocher A brownish yellow color.

perspective The art of showing three-dimensional objects on a flat page, creating the effect of depth or distance.

Pop Art (mid-1950s–1960s) An art style that celebrated the bold, bright images of advertising, cartoon strips, and modern life.

porcelain A white, clay-based material that is used to make china (or ceramics).

portrait A painting, sculpture, or other artwork that shows an image of a particular person.

print A way of transferring an image from one surface to another. Prints are often made by spreading ink over a raised or engraved design and then pressing it onto paper. This makes a reverse image that can be reproduced many times.

proverb A short, popular saying that contains a message or piece of advice.

Prussian blue A deep, dark blue color, sometimes known as Berlin blue or iron blue.

screen print A print made by dragging ink over a stencil marked onto a silk screen. The ink goes through tiny holes in the silk that aren't covered by the stencil.

sculpt To make three-dimensional art, called sculpture. Carving and clay modeling are both types of sculpture.

sculptor An artist who makes sculpture.

serjeant painter A highly honored artist employed by the British royal household.

silhouette A picture of something that shows the shape and outline only, usually colored in black.

sketch A rough drawing or painting, often made to help plan a final artwork.

smock A loose type of shirt, worn over clothes to protect them.

stencil A template that allows paint or ink to go through the holes but blocks out other areas.

studio A place where an artist or photographer works.

Surrealism (1924–1940s) An art style that explored the world of dreams, the imagination, and the "nonthinking" mind. Surrealist works often show familiar things in unexpected or impossible ways.

symbol A shape or icon that stands for, or represents, something else.

symmetrical When one side of a shape is the mirror image of the other side.

tapestry The art of weaving designs in yarn or thread onto a stiff cloth or canvas.

texture The feel of a surface, such as rough brick or smooth glass.

three-dimensional (3D) Describes something that has height, width, and depth.

vanishing point A point on the horizon where parallel lines, such as the sides of a road, appear to meet.

vibrant Lively or bright.

INDEX

Picture credits